FLAT CAPS & MUFFLERS

Ian McMillan

Cartoons by Tony Husband

Dalesman

First published in 2016 by Dalesman
an imprint of
Country Publications Ltd
The Water Mill, Broughton Hall
Skipton, North Yorkshire BD23 3AG
www.dalesman.co.uk

ISBN 978-1-85568-353-2

Typeset in Sabon.

Printed in China for Latitude Press Ltd.

Contents

Dedicated to my Uncle Charlie, who always
wore a flat cap and muffler with pride,
whatever the weather.

Introduction

I wake up even earlier than usual on the 20th day of each month because it's a special day: it's Column Day, which is a bit like Monday but scarier, and a bit like Saturday but more relaxed. Column Day is the day each month when I write my words of the purest Yorkshire Gold for *Dalesman*.

It's a scary day because each month I think I won't be able to think of anything to write that involves Yorkshire,

and it's a relaxed day because after just a few minutes I realise that Yorkshire is infinite, and contains multitudes, and is a house that has many, many rooms in and so it's easy to write about Yorkshire, really easy.

In fact, nothing could be easier: I just reach into the endless fund of Yorkshire stories, memories, folklore and fantasies and I write them down. And then, and this is the bit that fills me with deepest happiness, I send the column off to the great cartoonist Tony Husband, who has to illustrate it with skill and wit. And the reason I'm deeply happy at this point? Tony is from Lancashire. And he has to make a Yorkshireman look good.

Enjoy this book. You too, Tony.

Ah'm from Yorksher, tha knows

There was this Yorkshireman, and this Yorkshireman, and this Yorkshireman and this Yorkshireman, and they were sitting outside a pub in the spring sunshine talking to each other about matters Yorkshire. This sounds like the start of a joke, but it isn't. To the outsider (the Lancashireman, say, or the Man of Kent) they are just four Yorkshiremen sitting on a bench, but to the insider (the reader of this book, say) they are four keepers of the sacred vessels of some of the many different Yorkshire languages. Let's lean in and catch their conversation...

Listen to the man from South Yorkshire, although that could be difficult because since he's from South Yorkshire he's hardly speaking. Why waste breath on words? is what he's thinking. Thinking, note; not saying. The most he can muster is an 'Aye...' and when he greets his fellow bench-sitters he does it with a slight sideways movement of the head that's barely perceptible to the human eye. Why waste breath saying Heyop? is what he's thinking. You didn't need words down the pit. You needed all your breath for breathing.

Listen to the man from West Yorkshire; he's from a former mill town with a big old library and a number of Rugby League teams. He's got that endemic West Yorkshire loquacity and he's rattling away like a can of mabs. 'Now then Horace my old mate; I've not seen you since last

Cleckheaton Fair which as I remember was a day that began cloudy and ended up sunnier than my old Uncle Clem who had a smile like a set of chapel piano keys.'

Listen to the man from East Yorkshire. His face is lined from years of staring at the North Sea and wishing that it would warm up just a little bit, and that the wind would drop for just a second. He doesn't mind talking but he doesn't like to open his mouth too far as he does it in case his tongue ices up and his teeth freeze. This lifelong exposure to strong breezes has twisted his vowels like scarves on a washing line in a gale. He finds sterns in the rerd not stones in the road, and where others have a pint of mild at five to nine, he has a parnt of marld at farve to narn, opening his mouth just a fraction to sip and not glug. He will tell you that his way of speaking comes straight from the Vikings, and who will deny him with those horns coming out of his flat cap?

Finally, listen to the man from North Yorkshire. Listen hard. Listen carefully. He's talking a lot, almost as much as the wordy bloke from West Yorkshire, but his three fellow Yorkshiremen have great difficulty in following much of what he's saying. This is because he's using lots of words and phrases that don't really exist outside the small hamlet near the Latin Quarter of Crackpot that he hails from. He's right powfagged. He had to chase an old gleg across the moors this Noondawn. The gleg would have got away but it fell in a blatherdyke up to its hovvers. The observer might suspect that the man from North Yorkshire is making at least some of these words up, and the observer might be right.

Let's leave the four Yorkshiremen outside the pub, talking their way around at least four of the points of the infinite Yorkshire compass; and next time somebody tells you there's such a thing as a single Yorkshire accent, point out to them that's like saying there's such a thing as a single sunset or a single breeze ...

My wife's sister and her husband, Barnsley people born and bred, once decided to up sticks and open a pub in a small village near Stranraer, where the nearest big supermarket was a ferry ride away in Belfast. They hung bunting out and bought an A-board and put it near the road and opened the doors with a flourish, and stood there smiling, but for the first three days nobody came in.

Then, on the fourth day, a small Scotsman, wearing what they call a bunnet but what we call a flat cap, scuttled through the door. My brother-in-law could hardly see him over the bar. 'Are you an Englishman?' the bloke asked. Quick as a flash my brother-in-law replied 'No, I'm a Yorkshireman' and the wee Scotsman exclaimed 'That's all right then!'. That night the pub was full of him and his mates drinking pints and chasers and showing my sister-in-law how to deep fry a Kit-Kat without taking the wrapper off.

This little story teaches us that Yorkshireness is more than an accident of birth and an ability to whip up a Yorkshire pudding because you've got Yorkshire wrists; it's a state of mind and an identity that can, I reckon, go far beyond any national ties. When I'm at Oakwell watching the mighty Barnsley FC, and we're playing a Lancashire team, Preston, perhaps, or Burnley, their supporters still come out with the old chant 'Lancashire, tralala/Lancashire, tralala' to which we reply with the single word 'Yorkshire! Yorkshire! Yorkshire!' as though the repeating of the word with the rhythmic force of Deep House music will actually (and perhaps it has, I've never checked) force the Lancashire types to renounce their Lancashireness and come over to the county where the sun always shines and the Christmas cake is always served with a little slab of cheese.

Non-Yorkshire types, people from counties like, say, Staffordshire or Avon, often accuse us of arrogance, of a kind of blunt brussen-ness that bulldozes the feelings of anybody not fortunate enough to come from one of the

Ridings. I'm sure that's not true, although I do remember once going to see Yorkshire play Leicestershire at Headingley, and Yorkshire weren't doing very well, and a man with more tattoos than skin who'd been out in the sun too long, stood up and shouted 'Come on, Yorkshire: they only make shoes!' and got a round of applause from the rest of us, who'd all been out in the sun too long.

So what is this quality of 'Yorkshireness' and how can we really define it? I've mentioned already the ability to whip up a good Yorkshire pudding and the strange compulsion that drives us to reach for the cheese whenever the Christmas cake comes out, but it must be more than that.

I'm sometimes asked by the national media, at times like Yorkshire Day, what defines the essence of Yorkshire and in the end I often come down to the fact that we seem to have an oppositional quality. We don't take things for granted. We don't swim with the prevailing tide. We think for ourselves.

And there must be something in the way we stand. Years ago I was in Newark Airport, New Jersey, waiting for a plane back to Manchester. I wasn't wearing a flat cap or a muffler and my hand luggage didn't include a whippet, but as I sat flicking through my *New York Times* a man came up to me and said 'Does tha know how Barnsley went on at t' weekend?' and I said I didn't, and how did he know I was from Yorkshire? He looked dreamy and mystical, which could have been the effect of the beer he'd been supping, and said 'Tha can just tell'. I agree. I'm not an Englishman. I'm a Yorkshireman. Now, where's that cheese?

I'm often amazed when people, in trying to defend Yorkshire's reputation and trying to thrust it into the twenty-first century on a surfboard made of broadband internet connections, say 'It's not all flat caps round here, you know', as though the flat cap is the equivalent of a scold's bridle or a ducking stool, as a symbol of a long forgotten era. Well, let me tell you that I'm here to defend the flat cap, on as many levels as you like. It's a cultural symbol, it's a historical artefact, it's a piece of living craftsmanship and it keeps your head warm. It just doesn't suit some people, that's all.

When I was younger, every man on the street wore a flat

cap; at football matches it looked like a huge gang of extras had all turned up for a film called 'Trouble at t' Mill', and when a bus disgorged its passengers all you saw were caps and mufflers and overcoats. Sometimes not the overcoats, actually, depending how hot the summer was. And nobody ever called the flat cap a flat cap; it was always just a cap. We all knew they were flat. We weren't as daft as we looked, which was a good job.

If you flew above any Yorkshire town during a slight drizzle you wouldn't see any bare heads. You'd just see a phalanx of flat caps and a sea of rainmates glittering with water. Ah, the rainmate: don't get me started on rainmates, the female equivalent of the flat cap, the handy foldable device that kept the splashes off your mother's perm when she'd just been to the hairdressers, and which women often wore as a preventative; 'It looks like rain,' Auntie Winnie would say when I asked her why she was wearing her rainmate on a sunny day. And somehow, because she wore it, the rain held off. Voodoo, I call it.

So there comes a time in every Yorkshireman's life when he has to decide when he should wear his first flat cap. I was born in 1956 which means that by the time I was a teenager and at grammar school, a lot of my mates were going down the pit and wearing a flat cap as they boarded the pit bus. I stayed on at school and went to polytechnic in Stafford, which delayed the flat cap decision for a couple of years, but then when I came back to live in Yorkshire I felt it was the right time to wear one. I would wear it ironically, of course. It wouldn't be a flat cap, it would be a '*flat* cap', or even a 'flat *cap*' so that I could stand out in the bus queue as a college boy and not National Coal Board fodder.

I went to an old-fashioned shop and tried a couple on. Some made me look like my Uncle Les. One made me look thirty years older than I actually was. I tried a white one on, thinking that I looked like Robert Redford in The Great Gatsby. The shop assistant was enthusiastic: 'Natty as a carrot,' he said. My girlfriend, who is now my wife, was scathing. 'You look like a children's entertainer who can't get any work,' she said. I put the cap back and, in a bad mood by now, picked up a black one. I tried it on. I looked Bohemian and raffish. I looked like a Yorkshire Beat Poet. I looked cool. I bought it. I noticed that my girlfriend was giggling. I wore it once. At the bus stop somebody said 'Couldn't tha get a proper cap?'. I took it off and

screwed it angrily into my pocket, deciding against explaining the concept of irony. When I got home I put it in a drawer, where it sat for many years, until I got it out again in the early 1990s.

I looked at myself in the mirror. I looked stylish. I looked ironic. I looked like I was making some kind of statement. I came downstairs. My wife and three kids stared at me. They held their mouths until they couldn't hold the laughter in any longer. They exploded with hilarity. Eventually my oldest daughter asked me, gasping for breath, if I'd joined a soul band. I screwed up the cap again.

But now, maybe it's time to bring it out once more. What do you reckon? It's either that or my old rainmate.

Special greetings to those born in the Year of the Cap, particularly those born towards the neb end of The Year of the Cap. The reason I'm talking about years of caps and neb ends is because recently, while doing a bit of research for my PhD on Brown Sauce as Cultural Signifier in the Dearne Valley, I came across a fifteenth-century manuscript entitled Nathaniel Micklethwaite's Boke of Yeeres in which the eponymous Nat had set out a scheme for describing years in certain ways, in a seven-year cycle a little bit like the Chinese years of the dragon, the pig, the ox, the rabbit and half an arkful more.

So following Nathaniel's mathematical divinations, I can tell you that 2011 was the Year of the Cap. Anybody born in this year is, in effect, a typical wearer of the flat cap. You know the kinds of people I mean: you've seen them on the beach at Scarborough in the height of summer, surrounded by people in shorts and bikinis. They kept their cap on, even though they might have allowed themselves a short-sleeved shirt and sandals. The cap is firmly stuck to the head. It might be a summer one, of course, white as a new vest, but it's still a flat cap. After all, it might rain. After all, it might turn that bit colder. After all, they don't want their bald bit burned. It symbolises caution, lack of adventure, a why-go-abroad-when-we've-got-Brid attitude.

According to Micklethwaite's Boke, 2012 was the Year of the Whippet, and that's another matter entirely. Anybody born in a Whippet Year is, like the whippet, fast. Again, you've seen 'em. Sit at Skipton station at commuter time and watch the whippets running for the train, always just in time, no point being early because they wouldn't want to miss their five-mile run before breakfast, getting to the platform just as the Leeds train is rattling in, leaping urgently into their seat and speed reading the free paper as fast music hisses on their iPod. It's appropriate for the year of the Olympics, of course; we could get a few Whippets in the Yorkshire team. Will knurr and spell be an Olympic Sport by then? Hope so.

2013 was the year of the Yorkshire Pudding, and people born in that marvellous year are, like the Yorkshire pudding, much greater than the sum of their parts. Consider the ingredients of the pudding: flour, eggs, milk. And then consider the alchemy of the mixing, the wrist action, the batter-bubbles, the hot fat, the hot oven, the rising of the puddings like the sun coming up on a spring morning. That's what a pudding-year person is like: more complex

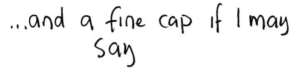

than their raw ingredients. Again, you'll have met them. The cello-playing window cleaner, the chubby bloke who can swim faster than anybody in the pool, the woman who can work out complicated mathematical formulae without the use of fingers, thumbs, toes or calculator. Yorkshire puddings, the lot of them. He spoke a lot of truth, that Mr Micklethwaite.

There are other years too, of course, and no time to go into them here. Year of the Parkin: its people are crumbly, but with a bit of an edge. Year of the Muffler: these people are like Flat Cap people, but even more so. Year of the Pigeon: these people never move far, but if they do, they always come home.

And what about the question of mixed marriages? What if a Flat Cap married a Whippet? What would they do in the evenings? Would they sit on the settee with their noses in a book they'd read fifteen times before, or would they be rushing round the house with a Hoover after a session at the gym? Intriguing questions.

If you want to work out who you are, here's the list. It goes in a seven-year cycle, just work backwards.

2011 Cap
2012 Whippet
2013 Yorkshire Pudding
2014 Parkin
2015 Muffler
2016 Pigeon
2017 A Nice Cup of Tea

My wife and I were walking through Liverpool the other day when we noticed two blokes in flat caps and mufflers strolling towards us, deep in conversation. 'Here come two Yorkshiremen far from home!' I said, but her antennae are much sharper than mine (and bigger, shinier, and more brightly coloured: that's why she wears a hat). 'They're not from Yorkshire,' she said, confidently, and she was right; as we passed them we could hear they were chatting away in Liverpool accents as deep and meaty as a bowl of scouse.

If you ever see a Yorkshireman listening, he's probably dead

Later, over a cup of tea, we tried to work out what it was about the two chaps that marked them out as non-Yorkshire, despite the fact that from a distance they looked prime Yorky stock, with the flat caps and the mufflers. I was baffled but my wife had the answers. She pointed out that both of them had their caps on at a very slight angle, just this side of jaunty, and when I thought about it, she was right, and that was why they couldn't possibly be from the White Rose County.

The Yorkshireman always wears his flat cap dead straight, neb forward like the bill on a duck; worn this way, the cap is a symbol of the Yorkshireman's straightforward nature, his unswayable belief that, for example, Geoffrey Boycott is the greatest sportsperson (never mind the greatest cricketer) that ever lived and that, all in all, Rotherham has more to offer than Paris or New York.

If the cap is even a millimetre to one side then the Yorkshireman could be accused of frivolity or softness, and that would never do. My wife also pointed out that the mufflers weren't white. One of them was a kind of Elvis-quiff brown, and the other was the sort of green that the most delicious mushy peas, the ones from the very bottom of the tin, glow with.

Silly me: it was obvious! The true Yorkshire muffler is invariably a kind of just-off-white, the sort of almost-colour that the people who write paint catalogues call 'Misty White' or 'Topsail White' but which could be more accurately described as 'Yorkshire-Pudding-Mix White'. In other words, the typical Yorkshire muffler is one that began life, when it was bought for Christmas by Auntie Doreen from Wyke many years ago, as pure white, but over the years and washings and dryings and walks in the fog and afternoons at the football and nights at the pigeon loft, it's lost just a patina of its original whiteness, enough to render it something just south-west of white.

My wife sipped her tea and pointed out the most obvious clue that the two men we met weren't from God's Own Country. 'Did you notice,' she said, smiling at the memory, 'that they were listening to each other? They were waiting until the other one finished before they spoke?' I interrupted her before she had a chance to finish: 'Of course! That means they can't have been ... ' 'Yorkshiremen!' she shouted, interrupting me and not letting me finish.

Silly me again. Yorkshiremen never listen to each other; they give a semblance of attention but really they're not listening at all and they're just waiting for the other speaker to draw breath so that they can wade in with their two-penn'orth. The two men we saw in Liverpool were actually having a conversation, but if they'd been from

Yorkshire they would have been having two monologues, two stories without an audience, two threads of language that would never, ever meet. It would have been an anec- dote-duel, a marathon of not-listening, of not taking any notice of the other bloke, no matter how interesting his tale would appear to be to an outsider.

So there you have it. How to spot a Yorkshireman: Flat cap as straight as a ruler, muffler the colour we call 'Not Quite White' and engaging in verbal combat not conver- sation. Now just let me go and straighten my cap.

Occasionally, very occasionally, I've stood in the coun- tryside in somewhere like Scotland or Wales or, I admit, Lancashire, and thought 'What a fantastic view!' as I gaze at a sunset or an expanse of trees or a solitary heron standing as still as a model of a solitary heron. My second thought, after I've acknowledged the beauty of what I'm looking at, is, 'What a shame it's not in Yorkshire'. My third thought is: 'is there any way the thing I'm looking at could become part of Yorkshire ...?'. And then my brow furrows like a ploughed field and I stroke my chin and go 'Hmmm'.

And that's why I've invented a tool that will prove invaluable to those of us who wish Yorkshire was every- where in the world, all the time. I call it StealthYorkshire and it looks like a cross between a screwdriver and a fancy fountain pen. It'll take a while, decades perhaps, but with the aid of this device Yorkshire will soon not only be the biggest county, it will be the only county.

It's simple, really; next time you're somewhere in the

borderlands of Yorkshire, like Todmorden or those areas at the far side of Rotherham where the county bumps into Nottinghamshire, you'll be able to use the device. Take a map with you and note just where the border is. Stand on the border and point your StealthYorkshire at the invisible line on the ground that separates Yorkshire from everywhere else. Press the button at the tip of the StealthYorkshire. A humming noise, similar to that made by your dad as he slept or your old valve telly just before it blew up, will be heard. Then a geographical miracle will happen.

I can't reveal too much at this point because of the delicate nature of the science involved, but suffice it to say that a ray will leave the tip of the StealthYorkshire and subtly move the border a few centimetres. Perhaps half a metre. Perhaps, if the battery is fully charged, a metre. More than that and the power diminishes and, frankly, the people of the neighbouring counties begin to get suspicious. Imagine a border between counties as being a bit like the boundary rope at a cricket ground; all the StealthYorkshire does is shift it a little.

The implications are enormous for those of us who love Yorkshire. Perhaps a member of your family has moved to just within the Lincolnshire boundary but they (and you) want to remain denizens of God's Own Country. Simply visit them over a number of weeks with your StealthYorkshire in your hand and over time they will transform from Yellowbellies into Tykes. Their vowels will flatten. They will feel the need to make and eat Yorkshire puddings before every meal rather than the frankly sickly Lincolnshire cakey. They will feel drawn to Brid not Skegness.

I'm thinking that if enough of us buy the Stealth Yorkshire we could use next year's Yorkshire Day to make a concerted effort to enlarge the county. Let's station ourselves at every point of the border. Let's, at a given signal from someone like Dickie Bird, switch our Stealth Yorkshires on. Let's feel the power. Let's feel the love. Let's feel Yorkshire spreading like a stain or spilled tea on a tablecloth. Let's take our StealthYorkshires on holiday and claim places like the Eiffel Tower and Times Square for Yorkshire. You'd just have to walk round the base of, say, the Pyramids, with your StealthYorkshire switched on, and they would be an island of Yorkshireness in a desert of, well, desert.

People might say the StealthYorkshire would never work, but remember you heard it here first. And they said the steam engine would never work. They said the telephone would never work. They said the Cleckheaton Thrush-powered Tram would never work. Well, it never did. You just couldn't get the thrushes to fly straight. But the StealthYorkshire is another thing entirely.

Happy New Year to you all (of course, you'll have to save reading this page until the beginning of January or just pretend Christmas has recently passed). This is the time of year when we all start to think about resolutions and I've come up with the perfect one for all Yorkshire Folk: I Resolve To Make Up A New Yorkshire Word Every Week And Use It Until It Gets Into The Dictionary. All together now: 'We resolve ...' The reason for this is obvious: Yorkshire dialect is a changing and shifting thing, a beautiful linguistic butterfly flitting from muckstack to farmyard via a weaving shed or two and a school play-ground in the morning sun. It's not a body of words set in stone, even Yorkshire stone, so it should be our duty as cit-izens of the county to refresh the dialect as often as we can to stop it getting dry and dusty. Or dry and gloffy, as they say in Muker. No they don't: I invented it, but you get my drift.

So, I'm creating one new word a week and saying it until I'm blue in the face and until other people start to say it too. I've got two words on the go at the moment, words that seem particularly appropriate at this chilly time of year, when the Christmas decorations have been packed away and all we've got to look forward to is February. The first word is 'flizzy' which describes a morning that has begun with frost but which has later turned to drizzle with a little bit of mist. It does what all good dialect words do

by using a couple of syllables when normal language uses quite a few.

What I'd like you all to do, as people committed to the future of Tyke Talk (we don't want it to go the same way as Latin, do we? As we know, Latin is now only spoken in the emptier parts of rural Lancashire – *Slippo Footov Stairsum* as they say round there), is to use 'flizzy' at least once a week to introduce to what we Men of Words call General Discourse. 'It's a bit flizzy this morning, isn't it?' you could say as you queue up for your tripe and cowheel at the butcher's.

Or you could mutter to your work colleagues in the office, 'By, I'm feeling a bit flizzy today', when you sit at your workstation and turn your computer on; they'll ask you what the word means and the process of language development has begun.

The second word I'd like you to shoehorn into your smalltalk is 'Paroom', which means 'I understand perfectly what you say but I don't agree with you'. So when some-body says 'I don't think Yorkshire puddings are as great a culinary achievement as cream of tomato soup' you can look at them with a quizzical eye, or two quizzical eyes if you can manage it without sneezing, and say 'Paroom!' and if you say it properly they'll know exactly what you mean.

If all readers of this book say flizzy and paroom at least once a week for the next year we'll soon end up with a healthy dialect that could run a marathon without getting out of breath. So now it's over to you: flizzy, paroom, and your own words, your own inventions and locutions to keep the Yorkshire language dancing and singing ...

I was walking through the Dales the other day, when I came across something mysterious happening at a place that must remain secret, so I'll have to call it Location X. It's just round the corner from Location Y, actually, across the road from Location Z. You probably know it. Anyway, it's a secret. Shhh. It was an odd sight; there were people digging in a ditch with tiny, tiny shovels and scrubbing away at the earth with small brushes. They were archaeologists, obviously, but what was unusual were the security guards stationed at each corner of the dig, talking urgently into walkie-talkies as I approached. I paused and glanced over at the site, and one of the security men motioned to me to move on. 'Nowt to see here, lad,' he said, in a voice like an Emmerdale extra, 'Nowt to see.'

I was about to protest when I realised that I recognised the guard; it was my old mate Trevor Bisby, the lad at school who wanted to be an airline pilot. Well, at least he got the uniform. 'Hello Trevor,' I said, 'what's happening here, then?' Trevor's eyes brightened; we'd been best friends at school and I remembered that his mother used to make some of the best parkin I'd ever tasted.

He lowered his voice and lowered the neb of his cap so the effect was like talking to a flower that had yet to come into bloom, and said, 'Can you keep a secret?' I nodded. He pointed to the hole in the ground and the people who were digging and brushing and sifting and scraping. 'There's something amazing down there, Ian lad: amazing and mysterious.' He let the words hang in the air for a moment like the smell of his mother's parkin used to linger in the kitchen. He was always one for the theatrical

gesture, which wouldn't have done him any good if he had actually made it as an airline pilot.

'Look down there,' he said. I saw dust. 'You've heard of the Great Wall of China, well this is the Grand Wall of Yorkshire.' I must have looked blank. 'The Great Wall of China is one of the most magnificent constructions ever made by man,' he said, sounding like a voiceover on a public information film, 'but this could be even more magnificent... '

It took a while to get the story out of him but it turned out that, some time in the ninth century, the people of Yorkshire (who at that time wore only loin cloths and flat caps fashioned from leaves) were suffering terrible raids from the people of Lancashire who would frequently rampage across the border and steal Yorkshire puddings fresh from the oven as well as whole plates of tripe and cowheel. Although they tried to resist, the Yorkshire folk proved powerless against the Lancashire cunning. Then, probably as a result of the Yorkshire Pudding Famine of AD 876, desperate measures were proposed by Stan the Unsteady, the King of the Yorkies.

He proposed a wall that would stretch the whole length of the Yorkshire/Lancashire border which would keep out the marauders or at least delay them until help arrived. This in itself was not a bad idea, but Stan's downfall was that he was a cook, not a builder, and he proposed building the wall from Yorkshire pudding batter, strengthened with rushes and withies. The Grand Wall of Yorkshire was mixed, cooked and set in place with great and triumphant ceremony.

Stan began his speech, standing on top of the crusty wall. 'Reyt, this'll keep them Lankys art on our territory,' he began. And the rest of his words were drowned out by a terrible thunderstorm; the heavens opened and rain poured down as though from a burst pipe. And, as Trevor said, the rest is history. The rain soaked the wall, the wall sagged and collapsed, the rain continued and ...

But tiny bits of batter and the odd withy survived, in Location X, and now they're being excavated and they'll eventually become one of the biggest tourist attractions in the North. But keep it under your hat: it's more than Trevor's job's worth.

When autumn's officially here and the nights are drawing in, I wonder if I'll see the Lights in the Sky again? I saw them loads of times last year, making their steady way across the dark in an odd kind of X formation. I'm not a believer in UFOs but I still couldn't fathom what they were. They certainly didn't belong to a plane coming down to Leeds/Bradford airport, and I'm pretty sure they weren't reflections of lights from a conservatory. Maybe, despite my scepticism, they really were intelligent life from a faraway planet, circling, orbiting, looking for somewhere safe to land their silvery craft?

And what better place for intelligent life to land than

A tells thee Seth... there is nowt
so queer as Lankysheer folks

Yorkshire? After all, we're teeming with intelligent life already, so a little bit more won't make much difference. Picture the scene: a September night in deepest Yorkshire and Old Seth is just taking his dog, also (for family reasons) called Old Seth, for a walk in the field by the woods. In the woods, a strange craft has just landed and an oddly shaped bloke in a silver suit has just climbed down a retractable ladder. He strolls out into the path by the field and strides up to Old Seth and Old Seth on his amazingly long legs. He raises a hand in greeting, and both Old Seths can't help but notice that he's only got three fingers, like Mickey Mouse in a Bacofoil jacket. 'Nah then, lad,' says Old Seth (the human one; Old Seth the dog can't talk. Not in public anyway), 'tha's gorra digit or two missin' theer! Esta bin in a ploughin' accident, like?' The silver-suited one looks confused, as well he might. He's been practising many Earth languages in preparation for his first visit, but he's not been practising Yorkshire.

Old Seth then does what he always does when people don't appear to understand him. He repeats himself very slowly and very loudly. He points to the extra-terrestrial visitor's hand. 'Ah seh, THA'S GORRA DIGIT OR TWO MISSIN' THEER OLD WARRIOR!' The alien feels confused but decides to speak. He speaks in the way he assumes English people speak, a cut-glass upper-class accent that sounds like chalk scraping on a board. 'Hellow! Larvely to see you!' he says.

He sounds like an extremely minor member of the aristocracy after a few hours on the sherry. Old Seth can't understand what the alien is saying, so he almost repeats himself again, pointing at the alien's hand again. 'THI DIGITS, KID. NOT ALL THEER!' The alien is flum-moxed. He tries again. 'Hellow! Larvely to see you!' Old Seth the dog begins to bark and now the alien is even more confused. Which of these strange creatures should he speak to? He leans over to Old Seth the dog and says his speech again, or tries to. He only gets halfway through the first 'Hellow!' before Old Seth the dog begins to bark so loudly that he tries to scuttle back to his spaceship. Old Seth the human says, in a kindly way, 'Dun't gerra cob on! He'll norrurt thi! He's soft as soooap that un!'

From the top of the steps of his spaceship, the alien makes one last attempt at communication, 'Hellow! Larvely to see you!' he chirrups. Human Seth is confused: 'I'm sorry old marrer tha just not coming through at all!' The alien holds his hand out for Old Seth to shake. 'Aye, I've noticed. Tha'r a bit queasy in't finger department ... ' The alien gives up and flies away, which is a shame because he'd got a huge sack of gold to give Seth, if only he could have made himself understood. Man Seth looks up at the disappearing ship and says to Dog Seth, 'Must be from ovver't hill. They're all daft theer. Or Lankysheer... '

Let's leave both Seths laughing like drains. I think I will keep an eye on the sky for those September lights, though. I could do with a bit of gold.

My dad wasn't a Yorkshireman, he was from the Scot-tish Borders, but when he left the navy he made his home permanently in the White Rose county. Him and my mam couldn't really have lived anywhere else at the time

The Scots toss the caber tha' knows

because she was looking after her ageing and sick mother, and my brother was only a lad and I was a toddler writing sonnets on a little chalkboard, but I often wonder why, later on, they didn't move to Scotland where my dad's family were.

Over the years I've developed a theory about that non-move, a theory that I've worked on over many long train journeys and evenings at home when there's nothing on the radio or telly. I reckon that, in my dad's tartan mind, Yorkshire was a superior version of Scotland so there was no need to go home. It was a kind of Scotland Deluxe or Over the Border Yorkshire. McYorkshire, if you like, or Scotland-wi'-a-Muffler.

Think about it: what do people say they like best about Scotland? The scenery. Everybody who lives in Scotland or who has even been there for a holiday talks about the mountains and the rivers and the wild moors and the little towns nestled in rolling valleys. Ahem. I give you Yorkshire, the Scotland of the south. You want rivers? Come and look at the Nidd. You want mountains? Will Pen-y-ghent do for you? You want wild moors? Stroll with me in the bleak uplands that lead inexorably to Whitby. You want little towns nestling in rolling valleys? Have you been to Grimethorpe lately?

What else do people talk about when they lavish praise on Scotland? That's right: the music. Flower of Scotland for example, lustily sung by tartan thousands at any and every sporting occasion. But how about Ilkley Moor Baht 'At, the greatest song of death and love and rebirth and duck cuisine ever written?

Okay, it's a bit of a dirge and it goes on longer than a bad sermon, but still. It may be a dirge but it's our dirge, and that's what matters. And here's another connection between Scotland and Yorkshire: if you sing the words of Flower of Scotland to the tune of Ilkley Moor Baht 'At, they fit. It's uncanny. And vice versa. Amazing. Try it for yourself. Go on, try it now, wherever you happen to be reading this book. Scotland and Yorkshire: two halves of the same coin.

Ah, coins. There's the other link. The myth of the tight Scotsman is only matched by the myth of the tight Yorkshireman. We've all heard the gags about the moths flying from the Scotsman's purse and the Queen blinking in the light as the £10 note is prised from the wallet of the Yorkshireman. They may be true and they may not be, but myth or not, the image of the miser binds us together.

Yorkshire is Scotland is Yorkshire: you just can't deny it. Finally, of course, there's the question of the national costume, and here it could be said that there aren't many connections. I disagree. You just have to delve. The Scottish warrior in full Highland regalia is indeed a stirring and frightening sight: the kilt, the sporran, the skean dhu down the sock and the claymore wafted in the air would strike terror into the quaking hearts of any enemies. And of course all the Yorkshire warrior has in reply is the humble flat cap.

I put it to you, though, that the flat cap is as much a terror-striker as any knife down any sock. Who hasn't quaked at the thought of a clip round the ear from the rock-hard neb of a cap wielded by an uncle? Who hasn't ducked as a flat cap has been flung across the room like a discus? Who hasn't found the eyes of his enemy shielded to the point of anonymity by the hugeness of his flat cap? Scotland and Yorkshire are united in battledress. So my dad was right; the two places are the same, reflecting each through the prism of the other. Och aye, tha knows!

I was wandering through a northern town recently and I noticed that a café was offering 'Traditional All-Day Yorkshire Breakfasts'. I mused aloud what that could mean, and a passer-by said 'Poverty and despair, pal' in a guttural tone that suggested he wasn't one of life's optimists.

I began to ponder: what is a Traditional Yorkshire Breakfast? And can you in fact enjoy it all day? The usual idea of a proper breakfast, and one that fewer and fewer people eat these days unless they're on holiday, is the fry-up with bacon and eggs and beans and tomatoes and sausages and mushrooms and occasional exotic visitors like black pudding and hash browns.

I was once staying in a hotel in Scarborough and I observed a middle-aged couple in matching leisurewear at the breakfast table. 'Shall we go continental, mother?' the husband asked, as though he was auditioning for a small part in an Alan Bennett play. He was glancing wistfully at a basket of rubbery croissants and some slices of baguette. She looked and sounded like the late Mollie Sugden. 'We shall not go continental!' she hissed. 'We did not come all this way on three separate trains to go continental!' So I

29

guess they had a Traditional Yorkshire Breakfast. And enjoyed it. Or else.

Maybe the Traditional Yorkshire Breakfast, or TYB, is like the Full English with Tyke trimmings: a little Yorkshire pudding instead of the black pudding, a bit of parkin by the sausage in a kind of sweet and sour melange. Perhaps the whole breakfast is encased in a giant Yorkshire pudding; no, that would just be toad-in-the-hole with style. Once, in a pub, I saw Miner's Lunch in the space where Ploughman's Lunch normally was on the menu. Putting aside the fact that no miner ever called his dinner 'lunch', it was always 'snap', I was curious as to what the Miner's Lunch would be, so I ordered it.

When it came, I thought they'd got the order wrong: there was a piece of crusty bread, a lump of indeterminate cheese, a flap of floppy ham, a pickled onion that looked like it had been taken from the nest a little too early, and a little pot of pickle. 'This looks like a Ploughman's Lunch,' I said. 'I asked for the Miner's Lunch.' The young man who'd brought it looked at my plate like he was trying to interpret a piece of art in a gallery. 'Sorry,' he said, 'I've brought you the wrong one. This is the Steelmaker's Lunch.'

Maybe that's the answer. Perhaps it's just a matter of language. Maybe the TYB is no different to any other cooked breakfast, it's just that if you mention Yorkshire then certain people will be persuaded to buy it. If something's Traditional then it's good; if it's Natural or Farmhouse then it glows with a kind of inner beauty. And if it's Yorkshire? Well, need I say more? It's bound to be excellent. However, my mate Dave pointed out that if you were in Staffordshire then any breakfast you had would be a Staffordshire Breakfast and in Leicestershire it would be a Leicestershire Breakfast. Now there's a marketing opportunity in these entrepreneurial times: if you run a café in Settle you could advertise a Traditional Settle Breakfast. When they sit down to eat it your customers might get a bit irritated by the fact that it just looks like any other fried breakfast, but then you would hold the logical high ground when you pointed out that any breakfast in Settle is a Settle Breakfast.

There's one more twist in the Traditional Yorkshire Breakfast story though, one telling reason why I didn't go into the café that morning and wolf one down. The café advertising the TYB was in a northern town all right: it was in Lancashire. No wonder that bloke said it would consist of poverty and despair. I moved on to the next café and went continental. After all, you can't be too careful. Especially over the border.

I'd like to extend a Yorkshire hand of friendship to readers from other parts of this country or from overseas who may not have visited our county before. Here I intend to provide you with vital information about your stay. You'll like it here. Now, a few tips to get you started in this happy and yet complex place that we call Yorkshire. Firstly, the correct pronunciation of the county is 'Yorksher' with the emphasis on the sher. Just imagine that you're sneezing and you'll be okay. Yorksheer is wrong as is Yorkshiyre. Yorksher is where you are, and Yorksher is what you should say.

Secondly, if you're going to wear a flat cap to fit in with the natives, always wear it in a serious manner. Irony will not be tolerated. The neb of the cap should always be forward and should never be slightly to one side. The flat cap should never be worn back to front in the manner of a rapper as this shows a lack of respect to the headgear of Yorkshire. Badges are allowed on the neb as long as they are in keeping. For example, an image of York Minster is acceptable; an image of Pamela Anderson running across the beach in Baywatch is not. Besides, you'd never get a neb that big.

When you greet natives of Yorkshire it's best not to be too effusive. This particularly applies to our French visitors; never, ever, go up to a Yorkshireman and kiss him on both cheeks. Even if you're married to him. This can lead to serious injury as the Yorkshireman will instinctively recoil from such intimate contact and may bang his head on a piece of furniture. A firm handshake will do the trick, but don't prolong the handshake as this can mean that you're betrothed in certain remote parts of Littondale. I find that a simple 'Now then' and a miniscule nod is more than enough.

When you are faced with Yorkshire cuisine remember these simple rules: it's always either gravy or custard, never both. A Yorkshire pudding is a starter and should always be treated as such and should be half-drowned in gravy before you hack chunks off it and attempt to raise the chunks to your lips. Curd tart and parkin, on the other hand, will often benefit from a bit of custard but not too much: no half-drowning here. Just a simple splash will

suffice. Just remember never to put gravy on your curd tart or custard on your Yorkshire pudding as this will mark you out as a visitor. Another note to our French visitors: do not say *bon appétit* as this will send the Yorkshireman to the racing pages to ascertain whether you're talking about a horse that's racing in the 3.30 at Thirsk. It's best to say 'Get thissen stuck in'.

Remember that Yorkshire folk always like to talk about the weather, and always in disparaging tones. If it's warm it's too warm, if it's cold it's the coldest day there's ever been, and if it's wet they predict a flood of biblical standards. I realise that for some tourists the weather is something to glance at at the start of the day and adjust to accordingly; for the citizen of Yorkshire it's an obsession, a way of life, an overarching philosophy. If you're confused, just agree to everything the Yorkshireman or Yorkshirewoman says and you'll be okay. In fact, not to put too fine a point on it, if everybody across the globe agreed with everything Yorkshire folk said, the world would be a much, much better place. Sorry about that. Didn't mean to get on my high horse.

So, to recap: Welcome. Handshake. Straight neb. Gravy or custard. Get stuck in. By, it's warm/cold/wet/foggy. That's all. It's simple, really: enjoy your stay.

You don't see many phone boxes around the place these days, and when you do see a phone box you don't often see somebody inside it struggling to get their cardigan off while their braces dangle and their flat caps are braced at an angle that experts would describe as just the tragic side of jaunty.

Well, let me tell you this was the sight that greeted me the other day in a Yorkshire town that I won't identify. I turned the corner and it was like I was looking at a giant fish in a very small bowl. The phone box was literally full of a man with a red face and sweat streaming down his chops. Somehow he'd got the braces tangled up with the sleeves of his cardigan so he looked like a mime artist trying to represent an octopus struggling up the River Wharfe in bad weather.

In the background I could hear feeble cries but they didn't seem to be coming from the phone box; they seemed to be emanating from further down the road. I ignored those for the moment, though, because the chap looked in genuine distress and in danger of either suffocating or catching fire. However, I pulled open the door just as the bloke got his braces untangled and his trousers fell down. Oddly, the man was wearing tights. Red tights. And his vast blue underpants were over his tights. And I realised what I'd found. I'd stumbled upon the legendary and sel-dom-seen Dales Superhero, Yorkshire Man. I know what you're thinking: like me, you thought that Yorkshire Man had retired. Since the mid-1990s sightings had become rarer and rarer. There was the Muker Poodle Rescue in 1993 when Yorkshire Man turned up to help a family pet out of a hole in a field, and there was the Bell Incident of Burnsall in 1996 when he foiled a plot to nick the bell ropes

from the church. Since that, silence. Until now. Oh, there were rumours for a while of sightings on the upper decks of buses in Pickering and in leafy glades on the far side of Pateley Bridge but no real evidence that Yorkshire Man was still with us. I felt like I'd found the Loch Ness Monster or the last dodo. I tried to fish my phone out of my pocket to get a photo. Yorkshire Man turned to me and spoke.

'Can tha gi' me a hand wi' me cape?' he said, in a voice like gravel. 'It's in my gansey pocket, folded up, like.' Up close, Yorkshire Man looked really ancient; his teeth looked like lumps of rotten banana and his face was as wrinkled as a screwed up bit of notepaper. I helped him on with the cape. The feeble cries I'd heard before seemed to be getting louder. 'There's an old lass stuck up a tree,' Yorkshire Man said, 'and I need to help her, like.' Somehow we'd both got entangled in the braces and cape and it took him ages to get out of the phone box. He stumbled across the road to a small tree where I could see a lady in gardening gloves stuck a third of the way up. To be honest, she could have jumped to safety, but she seemed to want to be rescued.

'Just fall into my arms!' Yorkshire Man shouted. And she did. And then she dusted herself down, blew her rescuer a kiss, and went back to her pruning. He returned to the phone box and laboriously got changed back into his cardy and cap. So keep your eyes peeled, especially near phone boxes. Yorkshire Man is still with us. I didn't find time to get a photo before he disappeared, though, so any photographic evidence would be much appreciated.

This is the little-known but very heart-warming story of the Little Dales Sparrow Who Tried His Best. It could be that older readers might remember their grandparents telling them a version of the tale but I think this is the first time it has ever been written down. As far as I've been able to make out, the events in the story are true and took place in the late 1880s. It'll give you a bit of a glow on a chilly February day, I promise. Here goes:

There once was a little sparrow who lived right in the heart of the Yorkshire Dales. This sparrow looked just like any other sparrow except for the twinkle in his eye: it was a twinkle that glowed like a star, a twinkle that promised fun, mischief and the kind of logical and imaginative intelligence normally denied to sparrows. One February day the little sparrow was flapping his way over the village of

Botherton-by-Botherbrough in Botherdale when he saw something happening by the village pond.

It had been a cold winter and the pond had been frozen since late November; for months the people of Botherton-by-Botherborough had been using the pond as a short cut across the village because the local vicar, an amateur scientist, had tested the ice with an iceometer (his own invention) and found it to be nineteen feet thick, so there was no chance of anything slipping through as there was, in fact, no water beneath the ice, just ice itself.

The Little Dales Sparrow Who Tried His Best noticed what appeared to be somebody breakdancing on the ice. I realise that breakdancing hadn't been invented at the time this story takes place, and that the Yorkshire Dales are not much like the birthplace of breakdancing, the Bronx in the late 1970s, but it's the nearest visual equivalent I can think of. A man in a uniform was slithering about on the ice, trying to stand up and failing, skittering over the pond's frozen surface like a beetle, doing handstands and forward rolls, standing on one leg like a heron in glasses then falling to the ground as though someone had tied string around his legs and was pulling it sharply.

The unfortunate slipper was Bert the Postman, who was a proud representative of Her Majesty Queen Victoria's Penny Post and who always got the post (first, second and third deliveries as they had in those days) through. He had been worried about being late with his sack of mail and so had rushed onto the pond a little too quickly and had, despite his stout boots, slipped. And now Bert couldn't stand up. He'd dropped his bag and the letters were sliding all over the pond like rectangular lilypads. And now the post was going to be very late and Queen Victoria would be displeased.

The sparrow could see that Bert was upset and flew down through the February air to try to help. Obviously, the Little Dales Sparrow Who Tried His Best was too small and weak to lift Bert up, but he did the next best thing: he delivered the post.

It's hard to believe, but it's true. For the next three hours, as Bert flapped and flopped on the ice like a hake with Post Office badges on, the sparrow delivered the post all over the dale. It took a while but, as his name implied, he Tried His Best. The villagers soon caught on to what was happening and they stood on the streets and cheered and cheered the sparrow.

The village brass band came and stood by the pond and played a fanfare each time the sparrow picked up a letter. Bert eventually managed to crawl off the pond by using spare stamps as sticky stepping stones and he thanked the Little Dales Sparrow Who Did His Best. Sadly the sparrow had delivered all the letters to wrong addresses and so Bert got the sack.

Moral: always ignore helpful sparrows.

In the dark depths of January, I was talking to somebody on a late evening train. It was a late late evening train, as well, getting later and later in the snow and the cold. In fact, further on in the journey it conked out completely with a groan and a hiss, so it became a late late late evening train. Me and this other bloke were bemoaning the fact that it was winter and, to try and inject a bit of light into the dark carriage, I said, plucking a month out of the air, 'Oh well, never mind: soon be April.'

He turned to me with a face that looked like it had been drawn on the front of a skull by a child. 'Aye,' he said in a Yorkshire accent so pronounced you could have made parkin with it, 'but yer can often have bad Aprils, can't yer.' The train ground to a halt and expired.

He's right, though: you can often have bad Aprils, and freezing Mays, and Junes that you could build snowmen in. He's also right because he was striking what I call The Yorkshire Attitude. Some would call it cynicism or pessimism but to me it's just The Yorkshire Attitude, or TYA for short. It differs from pessimism or cynicism because it

Grandad.. tell me again about tha bad Aprils tha's known

always has a twinkle in its eye. It's complex, is TYA; it's complex and layered and nuanced. Never tell a person from Yorkshire about the complexity and the layering, though. They'll glance at you with a look of pure TYA and say, 'Layered? I thought cakes were layered.'

TYA is a frame of mind, a mode of thinking, a manner of speaking. Everybody from Yorkshire reading this piece will be nodding because they know what I'm talking about. People who aren't lucky enough to be from Yorkshire will be shaking their heads and wondering what I'm on about. And that's because they haven't got TYA. They might have TLA, which is no good at all, or TNA, which is feeble. But don't tell the people from Lancashire or Northamptonshire that. Well, you can if you like, I'm not bothered. I've got TYA.

So, how can we define TYA for future anthropological and cultural historians? Well, for instance, when a person from Yorkshire tells you that you can have bad Aprils they're just setting themselves up for disappointment. In their heart of Yorkshire hearts they'd like April to be warm and welcoming. They'd like to walk about in shorts. They'd like to, if nobody was looking, gambol like a lamb. A Yorkshire lamb, of course, with TYA. But they don't want to admit that, so they prepare themselves for the worst by murmuring about The Bad Aprils, which sound like a band who did a couple of gigs round Ecclesfield in the mid 1990s and then folded.

If your birthday is in April you might open your presents with TYA and say 'I bet it won't fit!' or 'I bet I've already got one!' even before you open it. And when you open the present and it's a lovely jumper you'll say, with resounding TYA, 'Who knitted this? Lord Nelson?' which, to anybody else, would be insulting, but to anybody who understands TYA is praise indeed. If you're reading this as you have your tea you'll be saying, to anybody who'll listen, 'I bet I'll spill me tea on t' book, and it might improve that Ian McMillan if he gets soup on his sentences!' That's tea with TYA.

So, enjoy April, but enjoy it with TYA. If it's sunny, remark that it looks like rain. If you're feeling fit, tell people that you think you're coming down with summat. If a relative comes to visit, tell them you were just off to the shop. And if somebody tells you they're looking for-ward to the summer, say 'Aye, but you can have some bad Augusts.' TYA rules.

I can't put it off any longer. It's T time. I don't mean it's time to put the kettle on or get the golf clubs out. No, it's Time to Talk about T. Let's make T the Tyke Talk of the Town. Let's be more specific here: we're not just going to be talking about T. We're going to be talking about T'. Yes, the little tadpole that sits by the side of the letter T and turns it into something else; in fact, let's face it, that apostrophe turns the T into summat else, and that's the difference. That's t' difference.

That little tear rolling down the face of the page is used by some people as a curly stick to beat us Yorkshire folk with, and by some people as a badge of White Rose hon-our, and by some people as a complete and utter misrep-resentation of that marvellous language that we call Yorksher.

42

I first came across the t' in print when I was a student at North Staffordshire Polytechnic in the late 1970s. To be perfectly honest, it was the first time in my sheltered life that I'd mixed with people from that fabled region of the country called The South. As far as I was concerned, south meant Chesterfield, and the occasional visit to my Auntie Mabel there. There were people at North Staffs from all over the place, and one lad, a kid from Buckinghamshire, decided he'd call me 'Trubble at t' Mill' for reasons best known to his southern self. He wrote it on a bit of paper and stuck it to the back of the seat I normally sat in for the sociology lectures. I didn't mind. It seemed to amuse him.

'Here's Trubble at t' Mill!' he'd shout when I went into the refectory for my cuppa.

The only thing that really annoyed me, though, about his parody of our dialect was the t' that he stuck in just before 'mill'. That T' was huge. It echoed round the room when he said it, going off plosively like a gun or a bird-scarer. I tried to take him on about it. I tried to explain that nobody in Yorkshire had ever said that T'; instead, there was a minute gap in the sentence, a kind of ghost t' where the t' would be if we said it. It was too subtle for him; well, he was from t' Buckinghamshire.

You see, for me the linguistic thing that is represented in print as a t' is beautiful and subtle and nuanced, partly because you can't really write it down. It's like the click in an African click language or the way the voice goes up at the end of a sentence when teenagers or Australians talk to you: you can't print it. People have tried over the years with the t' but none of the solutions ring true. In a Yorkshire dialect play I once wrote I represented it as just the apostrophe, hanging there like fruit: I'm going to 'shop. And that's almost it, but not quite.

In the past I've also tried showing it as an asterisk: I'm going to *shop, but that didn't work because it makes you want to glance to the bottom of the page for a footnote. I've tried representing it as a forward slash: I'm going to /shop but that just makes you think that the shop has got a sloping roof. I've tried using an exclamation mark: I'm going to !shop but that just makes you think something surprising and possibly frightening is about to happen in t' shop.

It persists, though, in books and newspapers, that pesky t', and I think it's time we got rid of it and replaced it with something else. A little drawing of a flat cap, perhaps? A round O like a Yorkshire pudding? I don't know. It's over to you, learned readers steeped in Yorkshire lore like the best dunking biscuits are steeped in tea. Or t' tea.

Oh well, at least we're not from Lancashire. They take holidays in th' Algarve and eat Toad in th' ole!

Of course, we here in Yorkshire have been responsible, over the years, for many wonderful inventions: Catseyes, the mousetrap, the Hansom cab and the guillotine were all dreamed up by folks from round here, and we're rightly proud of them. Well, here's your chance to swell with pride a little more, like a balloon or one of those puffer fish that suddenly expand like a bloke who's just packed up his diet, because I can now reveal another very important Yorkshire invention.

I bet you'll LOL when I tell you that texting comes from the White Rose County. OMG! Love it or hate it, the text message is a fundamental ingredient of twenty-first-century communication and I, for one, feel a little glow in my heart when I know it's been invented by one of our own. ROFL.

Bill Broadmeadow was a farmer in the Dales in the 1990s and he was known from the market cross to the far reaches of the old churchyard for his taciturnity. In fact, taciturnity is far too long and complex a word to describe Bill's lack of loquaciousness, as is loquaciousness. Let's face it, he was dour. He'd make a coathanger look chatty.

It's said he wooed his wife Irene with the immortal phrase 'Cuppa, lass?' and his speech at his daughter Molly's wedding was a terse 'She's thine nar, owd son' to the gobsmacked groom. The entrance to Bill's farm was on a sharp bend and he often had to swerve his tractor when he came out on to the main road to avoid a holiday-ing family in a Ford Focus, or a besuited business-person in a sporty number. He'd shout 'Watch!' or 'Gerrart!' or 'Shift yersens!' but it seemed to make no difference and Bill was frightened that one day someone, possibly him, would get very badly hurt.

So he started to make notices, writing them on those bits of cardboard you get in shirts, none of which he'd ever thrown away since the mid 1970s. That's the cardboard and the shirts. And the bags they came in, because he was a proper Yorkshireman. The notices reflected Bill's linguistic brevity and he stuck them on the trees at the side of the road near his farm. 'Slow darn', one of them said, followed on the next tree by 'Slow reyt darn' and then on the next tree by 'Stop, will yer!'. It wasn't that Bill was deliberately writing the signs in a mock-Yorkshire accent, he was writing them as he spoke, phonetically, and he reasoned that he wanted the notices to sound as much like him as possible because, as he said, 'then they'd know it was me as put 'em up'.

It just so happened that a newspaper photographer was on holiday in Bill's area a few years ago and when he came across Bill's sign 'Ter fast!' he took a picture of it. The picture appeared in a number of papers and magazines all over the world and before you could say 'Thart Speedin!' Bill's notices began to receive the attentions of enthusiasts of written ephemera; fans of signs, in other words. The signs started to get stolen, on a regular basis, probably to order. Bill would make a sign that said 'Deead Slow!' and somebody would have it and within a couple of days it would be in a trendy café in a market town in the south of England or a gallery in Laos.

Bill was running out of shirt cardboard, unlikely as that may seem, and so he started to make the signs smaller, tearing the cardboard in half and sometimes into quarters; because of this he had to write fewer words and this was where texting was born because Bill's signs started to look like texts.

SLW DWN he would write, instead of Slow Down, and BRKS N for Brakes On. These shortenings had the opposite effect to the one he'd imagined, as more and more of them got stolen. Then a cutting-edge media consultant (that's what it said on her business card, anyway) called Naomi typed the words of one of Bill's signs into her handbag-sized mobile phone, and sent it to all her contacts.

The rest, as they say, is history. And to this day, Bill doesn't know how much influence he's had on the world's habits of interpersonal communication. I won't tell him. Will U?

The other day I was on a train passing through Driffield on my way to Bridlington; it happened that I was reading a paperback book and for some reason, as I gazed out of the window between chapters, I riffled the pages just as my eye was caught by the word DRIFFIELD on the platform. And, for a magical moment, the name and the sound I was making with the book became one and the same. Driffield, Driffield, Driffield: the noise of the pages of a book turning rapidly in a confined space. As the train rattled through the landscape it made a kind of sense. To me, anyway. I've often wondered how places got their names and I've also begun to distrust the accepted historical wisdom of nomenclature, which isn't a sequence of words you get to type very often.

After a while, it dawned on me that really many of the villages in our great county were actually named by our clever ancestors for their onomatopoeic qualities. They weren't simply visually descriptive: they reflected a sound associated with that place or with something that had happened at or near that place.

I began to think of Yorkshire place-names and what they sounded like. There were quite a few bells, large and small. Hull sounds like a huge cathedral bell sounding out the hours. Tong is a smaller bell, maybe the sort you get on the door of an 'Open all Hours' corner shop, and Tingley and Bingley are little handbells calling in the kids at the end of playtime in a tiny school in the Dales. Dungworth, near Sheffield, is an old bell tolling in the distance, the sound fading away. York (groaned slowly and loudly) is the noise a middle-aged man makes when he gets out of a soft settee and oddly it's also the noise a middle-aged man

makes when he sinks into a soft settee. I'm speaking from personal experience here, of course.

Gawber, near Barnsley, is the sound of a yawn that becomes a sneeze, and Wetherby is the sound of a sneeze, one of those that you try (and fail) to control. Thorne is the sound of a yawn, one of those huge ones that erupts halfway through an important (to some people) afternoon meeting; one of those that you try, and fail, to control. If you want the sound of a sneeze that becomes a yawn, you'd better go to Dishforth. Make sure the '—forth end of the name is spoken with a wide open mouth.

Some Yorkshire names sound angrier than others: Drighlington, near Bradford, sounds like somebody banging on a window to tell the kids to stop messing about in the garden, and Bridlington sounds the same but with double glazing. Jump in South Yorkshire sounds like a command and Luddenden Foot sounds like the words of an argument as heard through the thin walls of a cheap hotel.

Some place-names seem happy: Hoyland sounds like somebody laughing, especially if you repeat it a few times, and it doesn't take too much of a leap of the imagination to say that High Hoyland sounds like somebody laughing in a high-pitched voice. Especially if you repeat it a few times.

Pateley Bridge is the noise the plates make when you pile them into the sink before you wash them up, and Mytholmroyd is the squeaking that wine glasses make when you clean them with a cloth. Belle Isle (in Leeds) is the gurgling of water going down the plughole; again, the effect is enhanced, like it is with most of these name/noise interfaces, if you repeat them as many times as you can before the other person in the room tells you to shut up. It's a theory, isn't it? But what the heck does Wetwang sound like?

If a television producer was to approach me and say 'I'm making a series of programmes about the glories of Yorkshire; what would you like to put in?', I'd reply, with a faraway look in my eye and a timetable in my hand, the single word 'Trains'. I'd reply with enough conviction to make the producer whip out a contract and sign me up on the spot.

Yorkshire trains: the phrase fills me with excitement even as I write this. One of my earliest memories is going up to the long-Beeching-defunct Darfield station with my mother to go down to Plymouth to see my dad in his final weeks in the navy; it would have been 1958 and I would have been two years old but I have a vivid photograph in my head of a huge, rumbling, steaming monster coming round a bend and a man in a hat waving a flag.

I guess the love affair with trains started there; and now, even if I'm only going from Wombwell to Meadowhall, I still lean out and strain my neck to see the train rattling in from Barnsley, briefly disappearing as it goes down the dip and then coming back into view which tells me it's time to grab my briefcase and tap my top pocket to make sure my mobile phone's still there.

We'll all have our favourite Yorkshire railway journeys, of course, and here are a few of mine: the run from Leeds to Ilkley, through Menston, Burley in Wharfedale and Ben Rhydding, where, even though the bloke opposite you is tapping on a laptop and there's somebody in the next seat

working out their next month's appointments on their Blackberry, you still get a sense of what it might have been like to take the journey in the 1930s in the days when everybody wore a flat cap or a trilby or occasionally a bowler hat; the line from York to Scarborough, particularly on a summer day when it's packed with families eating picnics too early, and getting far too excited and thinking they're nearly there when they get to Malton (which, incidentally, had one of the great station buffets in Yorkshire rivalled only, in my humble opinion, by the West Riding Refreshment Rooms in Dewsbury, but that's for another time, another day, another bacon sandwich).

There are the preserved lines, of course, run by indefatigable enthusiasts with dirt under their fingernails: the Keighley and Worth Valley, the tiny one at the Elsecar Heritage Centre in South Yorkshire, and the wonderful North Yorkshire Moors Railway from Pickering to Grosmont where the start of our Christmas was always a trip on their Santa Special through the frosty woods wreathed in steam, with the kids getting giddier and giddier (although not as giddy as me, I can tell you) as the elves (well, enthusiasts dressed as elves) got closer and closer.

The crowning glory of all Yorkshire railway journeys, though, has to be the one from Barnsley to Huddersfield. You can keep the Orient Express and the Trans-Siberian Railway, give me that heart-stopping moment as the train appears to fly over the fields as it crosses the magnificent viaduct just outside Penistone; let me savour the sense of the train-as-community-lifeline that you get as people get on and off with bags of shopping and fold-up buggies at places like Honley and Brockholes, and let me keep in my mind's eye for when I get too old to go on a train anymore the awesome view of Huddersfield you get just before you plunge into the last tunnel before Huddersfield station. All aboard!

I know that some of you reading this book will be first time visitors to Yorkshire, taking a glorious chance on what trendsetters call a 'staycation', having a week exploring the delights of the White Rose County. Perhaps you're from that fabled and mystical country called The South. If you are, welcome, and here are a few tips and hints on how to behave in Yorkshire, a little bit of Yorkshire Etiquette you can practise so as to blend in with the natives.

We Yorkshire folk always like it if our visitors make an effort to dress in our regional costume. We appreciate the time and trouble you've taken. So, may I suggest a flat cap that is just a little too big so that it flops over your southern ears. That's how we wear them round here. May I suggest a muffler, no matter how hot the weather. May I suggest that the muffler is just a little too long so that it flaps in the unforgivingly warm Yorkshire breeze. That's how we wear them round here.

May I suggest authentic wooden clogs, as big as narrow-boats and as wide as wideboats. May I suggest that, although the wooden clogs may take a little bit of getting used to for you, they are well worth the effort and by the third day you'll be performing clog dances in crowded shops. That's what we do round here. Optional costume extras include a toy whippet on a string and a toy homing pigeon on a long string. These can be awkward to trans-port around but, believe me, we'll appreciate the effort and the kind thoughts behind the action as you drag a toy whippet through a market town on a string.

In matters of language, we like it when people from The South make an effort. So, when you go into a shop, always shout at the top of your voice, 'Eyop me old flowers! Art thou all reyt this morning?' Try it. Try it now, as you read this book. Good, that's good, but it's not loud enough. We like to shout. As loud as you like. We also like to go up to strangers and just pat them a little on the head. If the flat cap has to be lifted to achieve the pat on the new acquain-tance's bonce, then that's fine. We don't mind. Remember: shout and pat. That's it. We'll love you for trying.

Other phrases that will make you blend in are 'Eee by gum' which, by law, a person from Yorkshire must say at least thirty times a day, and 'Ecky thump' which is best said in libraries in a piercing and shrill yell. Also, we Tykes

find it very amusing to point at any item in any shop and exclaim 'How much!?'. Try it. Try it now. Louder, that's it. Maybe a little louder. Perfect.

When it comes to food, please note that we only like a few choice items and these should be consumed to the exclusion of all other cuisine during your visit. Please insist, as we do, on having a Yorkshire pudding as the starter for every meal, including breakfast. If you're not offered a Yorkshire then you are legally entitled to demand one, using the time-honoured phrase of 'Ah'm not shifting till Ah've gorra Yorkshire darn me'. You can also eat parkin and curd tart until you feel bilious; indeed, the biliousness is obligatory and is an integral part of being a person from Yorkshire. If you are offered fruit, look at it suspiciously and shout 'What kind of Yorkshire pudding's this muck?'. Go on, try it, try it now. Marvellous.

If you remember these rules, you'll have a wonderful time and we'll welcome you in Yorkshire with open arms, by 'eck we will!

I like a nice cup of tea. In fact, not to put too fine a point on it, I love a nice cup of tea, and because I'm a proud Yorkshireman I take part in the Yorkshire Tea Ceremony several times a day, and I'd like to share it with you so that you can replicate it in your houses inside and outside of this wonderful county.

The Yorkshire Tea Ceremony, or YTC for short, begins several minutes before the actual making of the cuppa. It starts with a kind of vague anticipation, a feeling of tealess-ness, of tea-lack. It's like the feeling you get when you haven't seen your wife or your football team or The Great Escape for a while and you're looking forward to seeing them and, as tea fans know, the anticipation of the tea is almost as exciting as drinking the tea, just like it is with The Great Escape. And after all, we all know that Steve McQueen would have got over that wire if he'd had a nice cup of tea before he got on the motorbike.

So the anticipation swells and you utter the universally acknowledged cry of the tea-starved Tyke: 'By, I could do with a cuppa.' The 'By' is important and we'll return to it later. You put the kettle on, making sure not to fill it too full because, let's face it, you don't want to waste power, do you? Electricity isn't cheap.

You get the pot, and there's lots of complex linguistic stuff going on here. My mother-in-law always asks if I want my tea 'in a cup or a pot' and I know that she means a mug not a teapot. So you get the pot and it has to be a Yorkshire one, maybe one that you got at a seaside resort or a beauty spot. The older the pot the better the tea tastes, I always say. The kettle is coming to the boil, making steamy music.

Now, I know that lots of people, lots of tea purists, like leaf tea and so do I if I'm not in a hurry but most of the time I have to admit that my version of the YTC involves a teabag. Not only that, it involves a teabag hurled from a great distance into the hole at the top of the teapot. This is an essential part of the ceremony. Stand at the far end of the room. Pretend you're Fred Trueman galloping down the pitch to shatter an Australian wicket. Bowl the teabag. Make it land in the hole. Perfect! I promise you the tea will taste a lot better than if you'd (yawn) simply dropped the bag in. If you miss, try again. Take your time. This is tea we're talking about.

The boiling water has been introduced to the teapot and your pot is waiting for the tea. If I am in a real rush I put the teabag in the mug/pot. I leave the teabag in, letting the tea grow in strength until it could arm wrestle its way to a medal. Today I'm being refined and the tea is brewing or mashing in the pot. Wait, wait. There's no rush, no rush at all. Then, at a time only you will know, the tea is ready to pour. Ah, that glowing and unforgettable moment when the tea glugs from the spout into your pot. There is no finer sound, I promise you.

Now it's time to drink. I don't have milk or sugar because I want the pure tea, but of course those additions are up to you. And this is where 'By ...' returns. Lift the pot/mug/cup to your lips. Say 'By ...' in anticipation, in recognition of the joy that is to come, in acknowledgement that the moment the tea is drunk is one of the great moments of civilisation. 'By ...' again, if you wish. Sup the tea and go 'Ahhh ...'. Let's get the 'By ...', 'Ah ...' combination right. Let's not 'Ah' when we should 'By'.

By, I could do with a cup of tea right now.

Look, here comes the Yorkshire New Year, striding over the horizon with the misplaced confidence of the truly innocent. The Yorkshire New Year is bright and shiny and its eyes are sparkling like the best fizzy pop. It's wearing seven-league clogs and its muffler gleams like gold. At a certain point, as t' old year crosses over into t' new one, both years will pass each other, one on the way out, one on the way in. T' old one will look tired; there will be circles around its fading eyes. Its clothes will look threadbare as though it's just emerged from a skip at the back of a closed down charity shop and, worst of all, its ideas will seem as thin as its shirt. It was once young and eager like t' new one, but look at it now: a husk, a shell, a shadow of a once-vigorous twelve months. T' new one, on the other hand, will burst into January grinning from ear to ear with naive promise and brimming with brand new thinking. So this is what t' new one has in store for Yorkshire; hold tight because it's going to be an exciting ride! Not too tight, thanks. I didn't ask for the Northallerton Burn.

We might as well start as we mean to go on and then everything will flow from it: Home Rule for Yorkshire, an independent White Rose state, proudly allied to the United Kingdom but a separate country within it. We'll have the referendum plans drawn up before the end of February and I reckon we'll have the vote in September. If it's up to me, the ballot paper, like the one they had in Scotland, will be simple and to the point. It will say 'Reyt, yore lot: do yer want to be free or not? Aye or Nay?' and, with a bit of luck, as the leaves begin to tumble from the trees in the autumn, the Ayes will have it and we'll be free from the Yoke of the South.

I'll be voting Aye and my main point of argument to the fainthearts will be that once you get out of Yorkshire they don't have their Yorkshire puddings as a starter, they don't have cheese with their fruitcake and they think parkin is something you do in a car park. That'll sway them. I mean, how can you possibly eat fruit cake without cheese?

Once we've got home rule then things will move rapidly as the autumn progresses: we'll have our own currency before Halloween, built around the basic unit of the How Much and the Half How Much, which dwindles via the Quarter How Much to the Nowt which is, as you've probably guessed, worthless. Because all this is my idea I'll have my head on the coins and the notes.

Well, it's only fair. Because the Yorkshire economy is so vibrant thanks to the continuing Tour de France effect we'll get a good exchange rate with the pound sterling and the Euro although perhaps not such a good one with the Lancashire currency known as the FootOfOurStairs.

Where independence and currency lead, language is certain to follow and by Christmas we'll all be talkin' Tyke reyt. We'll be cumin ooam on t' bus and once we get into the house we'll lig on t' settee wi' a cuppa. Language coppers will roam the streets enforcing every Now Then and How Do, and handing out on-the-spot fines of up to 500 How Much? notes. Dual-language road signs will be erected that reflect the flinty and often impatient nature of Yorkshire language: Turn Right will become Reyt! Reyt Nar! Will yer turn reyt! and Men at Work will be transformed into Blokes shuvlin. Give Way will be translated as Hod On. Just hod thissen on and No Cycling will be written as Gerrof Thi Grod, a grod being a name for an old push bike in certain parts of Yorkshire.

Independence, language, currency: this is the breakthrough year. I can feel it here, and here. Unless it's cramp.

Readers, it's time to remember the most daring April Fool joke ever perpetuated on the innocent people of Yorkshire; the older ones among you will be nodding sagely at this point and the young people will be trembling because they remember the stories their grandparents told them. I'm referring, of course, to the Great Lancashire Border Shift of 1928.

Yes, I knew that would make you gasp for breath. The bare facts of this daring hoax are simple; in the March of that year, John Gawston, editor of the *Dales Gazette*, a weekly newspaper which had begun just after the First World War, was having to face an uncomfortable truth: circulation was falling rapidly. His star columnist Dan

'Tales from the Barn Door' Massingham had defected to the rival paper, the *Dales Times*, and his horse racing tipster 'Bar the Field' Branston hadn't had a winner since the decade began.

Things were looking bleak for Gawston and the loyal employees of the *Gazette* who'd served the paper through thin and thin. Staring from his office window at the magnificent view, which was one of the few perks of the job, the editor remarked to his secretary Doreen that on a clear day you could almost see Lancashire and so it was a good job there weren't too many clear days.

Doreen replied, in her impeccably logical way, that if Lancashire was closer you'd be able to see it more clearly, and in Gawston's razor-sharp mind a plan was born. He got his journalists together and informed them that, on 1st April, they would produce a special edition of the paper that would inform the readers that, in a bloodless coup, Lancashire had annexed much of Yorkshire by the simple but effective method of moving the border. The journalists set to work with a Will, which was a modern typewriter that had replaced the more old-fashioned Wisp, and on the 1st April the paper hit the streets. The delivery driver then got out of the van and picked the paper up from the streets and took it to the newsagents that were scattered all over the Dales.

The paper caused a bigger splash than Gawston could have dreamed about; because the spoof was so convincing, so well written, and because nowhere in the newspaper was it reavealed that it was a joke, everybody who read it believed it. The result was mass panic. After all, which

Yorkshire person would want to be in Lancashire? According to the map published across the front of the paper, Lancashire would seep all the way across the Dales and would reach as far as Ilkley in the north and Sheffield in the south. In a clever piece of cartography a finger of Lancashireness extended all the way to Scarborough which was henceforth to be renamed, in a cruel blow, Little Blackpool.

People abandoned their homes and the roads were crammed with terrified Tykes trying to get to the few bits of Yorkshire that hadn't been annexed. Tales that the Lancashire Army would be impounding all Yorkshire pudding tins and replacing them with Lancashire hotpot pots resulted in hundreds of tins being buried in gardens, many of which are still being dug up today. Sales of white paint went through the roof as valiant Yorkshire citizens stored it up to repaint their roses after they'd been dyed red by the Lancashire hordes. Many people became homeless, sleeping in fields and on branches rather than admit that they lived in Lancashire.

Gawston was overwhelmed and decided to print a retraction the next day; such was the anger of those who'd left their houses (and in some cases burned them down so that they didn't fall into Lancastrian hands) that he was sued for all his possessions and the newspaper had to close down anyway. It's a sad and salutary tale from Yorkshire history.

Breaking news: the Lancashire border is being shifted. And this time it isn't a spoof. Promise.

The spokesperson for Yorkshire autumn came to see me the other day in my poetic garret, the one I keep at the top of the ivory tower in my magic castle. Yorkshire autumn, in case you've not heard of it, is the marketing company set up to promote the idea of attracting visitors to the county in this, the chilly and misty season. 'You've had the summer, now suffer this!' was one of their first and least successful straplines. That's the entirely fictional strapline for the entirely fictional marketing company I'm making up for satirical and humorous purposes, of course.

He bustled into the room, and instantly outlined his strategy, which can be quite painful unless you've done the warming-up exercises first. 'We see you as the man who can poetify our campaign's language,' he said in a voice that had just a hint of Estuary English about it. I'd never heard the word 'poetify' before, not even in a satirical and humorous column. He opened a briefcase and spread some items out on the table. There were teatowels, T-shirts, baseball caps and balloons. My table top looked like a table top sale of tea towels, T-shirts, baseball caps and balloons.

He gestured at the items; 'These need …' he pretended to struggle for a word. 'Poetifying!' I chirruped. He nodded emphatically. 'With your gift for words and our gift for selling, we'll have the whole world beating a path to Yorkshire's door!' He snapped his fingers. 'I like that line!' he said, 'you can have it for nowt. First drafts by tomorrow morning, please!' and then he breezed out of the room with all the grace of the first double-decker leaving the depot.

I gazed at the T-shirt and tried to think autumnal,

Septembery thoughts. Outside the window, there was a chill in the morning air and just a vague hint of mist. The apples on the tree were ripe and ready for picking; indeed, as I stared, one of them fell off and rolled a little way down the grass. I turned to the T-shirt. I turned to my notebook. As a writer, I like a challenge, but this was a challenge with knobs on. Or rather, with flat caps on. Ah, there's an idea: the flat cap, the symbol of Yorkshire. And, more importantly, the symbol of Yorkshire that's been discarded over the warm summer months. Autumn is flat cap time.

How's that for a start: 'Yorkshire in autumn: Don't

Forget Your Flat Cap!'. Not bad, not bad. But it does suggest that it's cold in Yorkshire in autumn. 'Yorkshire in autumn: You Might Need Your Flat Cap!'. Better. More subtle. But are they looking for subtlety? It's only a marketing campaign, after all. It's going to go on a T-shirt or a balloon, not in a vellum volume with a slipcase.

I decide to go outside and stroll around the garden with a cup of tea in my hand, strictly for the purposes of research, of course; as a writer, even when I'm walking around staring into space and supping from a Yorkshire mug, I'm still working very hard. The brain's still whirring. That's what I tell my wife. Outside, the cool autumn air seems to tickle my head. Maybe I could do with a flat cap. I stand and stare around the garden; my breath floats autumnally in the air. Perhaps I'll nip back inside and grab a cap. I can't decide; I really can't decide. Maybe that's the point about autumn in Yorkshire; it can't decide either. It's ambiguous. It's the end of one thing and not quite the start of another. The nights are drawing in but you can still have long warm days. You can put a scarf on and discard it and put it on again in the course of a short excursion to the shops. I don't know if I'll need a cap or not. I grab my notebook from my pocket and scribble the phrase down: 'I don't know if I'll need a cap or not'. I glance to the window to see if my wife is watching me working hard.

'Yorkshire in autumn: You Don't Know if You'll Need A Cap Or Not'. I've just drawn it on the T-shirt. I've just written it on the balloon and then I've blown the balloon up. It works, I think. Let's see how it looks on the baseball cap, see if it feels poetified …

As a true Yorkshireman I'm always amazed when writers of novels, particularly writers from the south who probably believe that Yorkshire pudding should be eaten *on the same plate as the meat and veg and at the same time* (my italics to register astonishment and disbelief) rather than on a plate *before* the meat and veg as a kind of Tyke amuse bouche or starter, or invent ridiculous place-names for the Yorkshire towns and villages they're writing about. There'll be a brass band in Grimston, and a pithead dispute in Barnley.

There might be a cricket match in the picturesque village of East Gubberdale and a lifeboat rescue in Bothby-by-the-sea. We all know about J B Priestley's Bruddersford and someone clever once satirised that name Cleckhuddersfax, which is now the name of a West Yorkshire band. I guess I can see why they make these place-names up, particularly if they're going to be writing about the places in a less-than-flattering way, and it's a bit better than that nineteenth-century practice of writing 'I was waylaid by a cutpurse in the Yorkshire town of R-------M', but I still think they should use the actual place-names themselves.

Cleckheaton: what a marvellous brass band overture of a name. Wetwang: a name that exactly describes the mist on the fields by the main road of that charming settlement. Bradford: a solid name, a name built from industry and sweat and early morning mill hooters, especially when, in the Bradford way, you turn the 'd' into a 't' that's hardly there at all, just a hint of something inflected in the West Yorkshire air.

Then you get the exotic names, the names that the

Vikings left behind in the brims of their horned hats, or the names that baffled map-makers scribbled down as an elderly bloke in a cap tried to explain that this wasn't Upperthong, it was Netherthong '... and if tha gets thi uppers and thi nethers betwixt and atween then tha may as well go back to Luton.'

I once read a bit on a website about Yorkshire place-names regarding a presumably apocryphal place called Near Barnsley. Well, it suits me. You also get the short names, the ones that can be spat out like bits of that chewing bacca they took down the pit: Jump/Tong/Drax/Eske, and the names that are little Christmas-cracker jokes all on their own, like Friendly, near Halifax (Graffiti: Friendly Skins Rule If It's Okay With You) and Idle near Bradford, home of the well known, maybe too well

known, Idle Working Men's Club. And, of course, the aforementioned Jump, a small village near Barnsley (if not near Near Barnsley) which gave rise to the oft-repeated quip to long-suffering Yorkshire Traction bus drivers when I was a lad: 'Is this bus going to Jump? Well hold it down while I get on!' Ho Ho.

I wonder, though, if I was called on to create a new Yorkshire place-name for a TV series, maybe one about a postman in the Dales, or a milkman in the Yorkshire coalfield, would I be able to do it? Obviously, the names would have to have different qualities. The Dales village should have a wind-beaten tinge, it should be a name that would ring with the sound of birds if you held it to your ear, and it should be full of the lilting language of country folk. Nith. How's that. 'His early morning round took him in his red van through the main street of Nith.' East Nith, maybe? West Nith? Lower Nith?

And on the other hand, the coalfield village should have a smoky edge to it, a harshness and a sense of lost collectivism, a name that if you held it to the light would distort a little, would break into colours that tinged towards green and black. Gonthorpe? Gonthorpeness? East Gonthorpeness-with-Gonthorpe? I think I'll stick to writing columns, and leave the place-name people to the ancient people and the historians.

Let's zoom in on this Yorkshire seaside scene as the gulls wheel overhead shouting to each other in gull language 'I'll get his chips if you get his bread and butter!' just before they swoop. Let's focus on this bench somewhere on the front at Brid. Let's look closely at this holidaymaker, perched on the bench clicking a cheap biro.

He's your archetypal middle-aged Yorkshire holiday-maker. He's refused to go abroad because, as he said to his mates at the club, 'You can't get a decent cup of tea and when the weather's nice anywhere's as nice as here', and his mates nodded. He's been to a cheap clothing chain and bought some leisurewear, and he's proud of the fact that he didn't pay more than six quid for any item. In fact, the baseball caps were so cheap he bought three, much to his wife's disgust. He's had a nice couple of days, even though he's lost one baseball cap to the strong easterly winds, and the pint of local ale he had on the first night didn't agree with him. In fact, it strongly disagreed with him. In fact, it had an argument with him and it won on points. His wife would say it was the fourth pint that disagreed with him and that it was the fifth pint that made him put one of the remaining baseball caps on back to front and start rapping in the small bar of their licensed guest house, much to the amusement of a family from Sweden on their first visit to Yorkshire who thought he was performing a quaint old sheep-gathering chant.

And now he's on the bench in the biting wind clicking his biro because he's promised that this year, unlike every other year, he's going to send some postcards to his mates and his cousin Jim in Chesterfield who always sends him a card from his world cruises and his expeditions to the far corners of the globe. So our Yorkshireman, earlier today, marched into a shop and bought a dozen copies of the same card that happened to feature, right at the bottom corner and almost out of sight, the gable-end of their licensed guest house. He's marked the guest house with a big X on each of the postcards and written OUR LODGE in huge capitals above it.

That was the easy bit. He studies the back of the card. In a minute his wife will be back from the toilets and she'll be expecting him to have written at least one or two. He looks at the expanse of white card that he's expected to fill. On the one hand it's not a very big space; on the other hand it feels vast. He sucks the pen, which is a mistake. Well, it's his second mistake: his first mistake was to buy a cheap pen when he bought the postcards.

The pen explodes and he's suddenly covered in blue ink. He looks like an art event: 'Blue Man in Leisurewear. Mixed Media: ink and cheap cloth.' He stands up and

waves his arms, frightening a passing school party from Rotherham. He wipes his face, which is his third mistake, as the ink (how can so much ink come from a small clicky biro?) is now spread all over his head and hands.

Now his wife is returning from the toilets and she doesn't recognise him. She left Frank writing a few cards and now she's being greeted by an alien from the planet Blue. She screams. He waves and says 'Why did tha let me buy that cheap pen?'. Which seems unfair.

Overhead the gulls wheel and cry. Only eight days of the holiday to go. Wish you were here.

It's that time of year again

Ah, it's high summer in Yorkshire, and that can only mean one thing: it's time to go out and spot the Yorkshire people who can't quite work out what to wear. Let's go on to a typical Yorkshire street, shall we, and collect a few choice specimens and stick them straight in our album.

It's a hot day. The sun is shining like a new pound coin in a bright blue sky and the vapour trails from the passing planes are spelling out the word HOT. Now, who's that coming out of the paper shop? Yes, it's the bloke who can't believe, despite all the evidence to the contrary, that it's a hot day. He's wearing a thick suit. And a cardigan. And a tie. And a cap. He's sweating cobs. He looks like he's leaking or like someone has just chucked a bucket of water on him. Let's eavesdrop a minute on what he's saying to his equally overdressed mate, and what his mate is saying by way of reply.

'By, it's hot tha knows.'

'Aye.'

'I'll tell thee summat: it's not red hot, it's white hot!'

'Aye.'

You'll note that the besuited geezer's besuited mate isn't saying very much. That's because the adhesive on his false teeth is melting in the heat and he thinks that if he says too much his dentures will fly out and start biting the pavement. Let's leave the Perspiration Brothers to their

overheated stroll to the betting shop and glance at the man getting off the bus who is the absolute opposite.

He knows it's hot, and because of that he's decided to wear as little as possible. 'If tha's got it, flaunt it!' is his motto, but the problem is that he can, like the Great Wall of China (amazing how it's lasted so long when it's made of porcelain) be seen from space. He's a big lad. His back is as hairy as a welcome mat. His belly is the result of several decades of selfless dedication to the study of fine Yorkshire beers.

His nipples (sensitive readers look away now) are sticking out like chapel hat-pegs. His shorts were fashionable for twenty minutes in the late 1980s. His sunglasses make him look like a fruit fly. His sandals are the sort that Australians call thongs and, try as you might, you can't stop looking at his toenails. They remind you of something but you can't quite think what. Then it hits you: his big toenail looks like that mammoth's tusk you saw in a museum once.

The Perspiration Brothers pass the half-naked chap and the street is getting hotter; behind the specimens we've just discussed appears a man who is an amalgamation of the two. He's wearing a jacket, but it's a linen jacket, built for tropical climes. His trousers are lightweight and his shoes are not the bulky ones often preferred by Yorkshiremen. He looks okay, until your gaze travels north. He's wearing a white flat cap.

Let me repeat that, in italics for emphasis: *He's wearing a white flat cap.* I reckon it must be a brand new one, straight out of the bag, because it really is whiter than white. He's a danger to passing motorists if the sun catches it and reflects like a floodlight. I'm not sure what the white flat cap says, but I think it says 'I'm still a Yorkshireman tha knows, but I'm making a concession to that thing tha calls hot weather!' but to me it always makes middle-aged and elderly blokes look like extras from the film The Great Gatsby.

Let's leave them now: the Perspiration Brothers, the King of Flesh and White Cap Man. They look like a tribute band walking down this Yorkshire High Street. Yes, but a tribute band to what?

February sees a lot of Yorkshiremen, including the ones who can't drive, rushing into garages to buy flowers and chocolates. A lot of Yorkshiremen will be grabbing huge cards the size of protesters' placards from the shelves of card shops and then reeling at the till and saying 'How much!?'. A lot of sweating Yorkshiremen will be nervously turning and churning their flat caps in their huge hands as they stand in ill-lit lingerie boutiques surrounded by thongs and basques as alien to them as exotic fruit in a greenhouse; a thin assistant will be holding up something wispy and saying 'Is she about my size?'. The Yorkshiremen's faces will be as red as prizewinning beef tomatoes.

The reason for all this confusion in Tykes from Rotherham to Skipton is the arrival of Valentine's Day, and the need to mark the occasion in some way. My dad got it right without embarrassment, because he was an incurably romantic Scotsman; every year he sent my mother a card with a drawing of a stick man inside with a halo above his head like that old image of The Saint. It was understated, and it worked.

When I was first going out with the girl who's been my wife for the last thirty years, I thought I'd send her a Valentine's card; unlike my dad I had no style at all. I could hardly buy the card in question for laughing because I thought it was so funny. On the front was a picture of an old lady with the words 'You're the kind of girl I'd like to take home to Mother ...' and inside the hilarious gag '... she could do with a good laugh!'. The moment my wife-to-be opened the card was a moment I'd rather not remember, although it comes back to haunt me across the decades

during the sleepless nights. Let's just say it didn't go down well, and I haven't sent a Valentine since, which is a shame.

I think the trouble is that, as Yorkshiremen, we'd like to be romantic but we're not sure how. We want to make the big gesture and we want to make her exclaim with happiness but we don't know how to get from the idea to the execution of the idea. We rush straight from having a thought about what they'd like for Valentine's Day to completing the exercise without spending any time working out the consequences of the initial impulse.

You can see how the enthusiastic but ultimately romantically gormless Yorkshireman would work it out: would she like a ride on the back of my tractor? I bet she would! She seemed impressed when I talked to her about tractor driving on our first date so I bet she'd like to clamber on the back of my Massey Ferguson and I'll take her across the top field, the muddy one at the side of that really steep hill. She'll love it! I might even propose as we turn by the oak tree. Or: she told me the other night she'd like to be taller so I bet she'd like a pair of stilts from that new Novelty Stilt Shop up the Dale. I'll wrap them up so she'll think she's getting a clothes prop. You can get pink ones so they can be girly. She'll love 'em.

Our other problem, as Yorkshiremen trying to be romantic, is that we haven't quite got the words. I once overheard a man in a pub in a Dales village trying to express undying love to the woman he was with. The heartrending monologue went something like this: 'Seez. Tha noz. Er. Warrit is. Warrit really is. Er. Between us, like. Feelings and that. I. Er. Ah want ter say, like. Er ...'

Oh, just buy her a pair of stilts!

As the days get longer towards mid summer and the light streams through the curtains first thing in the morning to wake you up – if the singing of the birds hasn't done so already – the thoughts of every Yorkshire person turn to the Great Outdoors (of which we've got plenty in Yorkshire: let's face it, if you add it all up there's loads more outdoors than indoors) and whether or not this will be the year you get the tent out of the shed and knock the mildew off and go and pitch up somewhere miles from anywhere and yet yards from the pub and the fish and chip shop that are hidden behind the hedge.

There's something of the frontiersman in everybody from the White Rose County; we feel that we're close to land, that our roots are in the soil and that we like nothing better than to feel the wind in our hair, even if we've lived all our life in the middle of Leeds and the closest we got to the earth was when we fell down the front step last week because we slipped on a discarded paper latte cup. This is something to do with our proud history, I guess; it's a history of farmers and workers in the harsh fields and toilers in allotments and flotsam pickers on the beach. As Yorkshire people we think that the earth spins just for us, and the nearer we are to it, the more alive we feel.

At this time of year you see cars and bikes and hikers loaded down with camping gear as we try to get close to nature. Every camping site in the Dales and the Wolds and along the coast will be packed with families from Yorkshire's conurbations struggling with four-man tents like they're trying to take their pants off before they take their trousers off. A dad in a baseball cap will swear because he's left the mallet at home.

A teenager will cry bitterly because he's run out of batteries for his PlayStation and the camp shop is shut until tomorrow morning. A wife and mother in dubious leisurewear will be trying to encourage everybody to come for a walk by the stream, and a stoic grandma in curlers will be steadfastly making enough sandwiches to feed the whole of Heckmondwike.

I must not be a Yorkshireman at heart because I'm not really a fan of the canvas-and-tentpeg experience. If there's one thing worse, in my humble opinion, than packing up and going camping when there are perfectly good hotels with empty rooms and trouser presses just waiting for you, then it's the trial run, the night in the back garden in the tent with the kids prior to going off to a beauty spot for the weekend.

My brother did it once, on his own during a wet June in the 1960s. The overnight stay was fine but when he decided to cook his breakfast it became an epic battle with some Co-op sausages and my dad's old stove. The stove gave out as much heat as a school exercise book, and my brother sat gazing at the pink sausages for hours, as they turned slightly less pink and slightly more brown and the sun sank in the sky and a kid delivered the evening paper.

When my own kids were little I promised I'd spend the night with them in the tent in the back garden, even though I knew nobody would get any sleep and the sound of the birds and insects outside would make it feel like we were in the jungle. The night was set, and I promised I'd be home early. I'm not much of one for beer, but that afternoon I met an old mate and we had a pint. Or two. Or more. And a bag of crisps. I missed the last bus and had to get a taxi home. I staggered down the garden. There they were, in the tent, looking accusingly at me as I tried to steady myself on the pole. 'I'm sorry ...,' I said as the pole cracked and the tent fell in a heap and I landed face down in the grass. Well, I told you Yorkshire people liked to get close to nature.

Ah, November in Yorkshire: month of bonfires, and misty mornings when you can see your breath, and chills in the air, and the breathless writing of Christmas lists and letters to Santa. And, of course, the Marauding Mam with the Scarf and the Gloves. You know the mam I mean: your mam, my mam, everybody's Yorkshire mam with a scarf in one hand, a pair of gloves in the other and a glint in both eyes, shining through her glasses.

When I was little I thought that the function of mams was to keep you warm and make sure your hands were clean. Two questions peppered my childhood like choruses in some great drama, which of course they were: 'Have you washed your hands?' and 'Are you warm enough?'. The answer to both questions was easy. It was always 'Yes', and the reaction to both answers was always the same: disbelief.

So my mam (and your mam, and everybody's Yorkshire mam) marched me to the sink and made me do my hands again, and whipped out a scarf and some gloves and made me put them on, even if it was still oddly warm for November, even if the gloves made me sweat and the scarf tickled like mad.

I guess this tough love comes from a time when, if you didn't wash your hands, you caught something terrible (a bit like these days, of course, with Swine Flu hanging around like an unwanted cousin at a party) and if you didn't keep warm then you caught something terrible. When it came to keeping warm, the Marauding Mams were speaking from a time before central heating when big fat bolsters were shoved in front of doors to keep out the Siberian draught and everybody gathered round the fire to try and thaw the icicles hanging from the nebs of their frozen-solid flat caps.

So November comes as a bit of a surprise. You've had a lovely August, gambolling in shorts until late at night; in

September you got away with the odd cardigan and once or twice a woolly cap. In October you really had to battle hard not to put a vest on but by November the Marauding Mam was in full flight, brandishing the scarf and gloves like banners at a demonstration. A demonstration against cold weather.

And it's no good protesting that you're not cold. It's no good protesting that no other kid at school is wearing a scarf or gloves. It's no good trying to inform your mam about the phenomenon of Global Warming with the aid of maps and diagrams and power point presentations. It's no good pleading that you look daft in a scarf and that the gloves are too big. You can cry, if you like. You can sulk, if you want. None of it will do any good: the Marauding Mam has got you. She knows that Yorkshire in November is colder than the inside of a fridge, and she knows that it's her maternal duty, driven by instinct and knitting, to keep you cosy and warm.

November: month of the scarf, and the gloves. Then you know what's coming, falling out of the wardrobe in a woolly and thermal avalanche. The thick jumper, knitted by an ancient auntie from Skipton using wool so thick you could pick a double decker bus up with a strand of it. The balaclava, making your ears smoulder and the back of your neck burn. The winter coat made from cloth like that bratishing you used to have on the shed roof, bought by the Marauding Mam from a sensible shop with you in reluctant and moaning tow in the height of summer when winter clothes were cheap. The vest, thermal preferably. The hairy socks.

83

Look at Yorkshire's children in November: big fat scarecrows, bulked up by layers of winter clothing. Goodbye, knees: see you next year.

Winter, eh? How cold is it? Well, let's eavesdrop on this gaggle of Yorkshire types waiting for the Post Office to open in the thin and harsh February air somewhere in the Dales. Some of this motley group are stout, some thin, some mardy, some affable, some just the affable side of mardy, some just the mardy side of affable, but all of them cold. But how cold? Have a listen.

George speaks first, his breath coming in huge steamy froths, like sheets billowing on a line. 'It's cold as the inside of my fridge,' he says. The others nod. They know that's just for starters, they know there's more to come. George's mate Cyril pipes up: 'It's colder than our Ethel's heart,' he wheezes. Some of the group gasp. The ones who knew Ethel.

George takes this as a challenge. I would say he was warming up, but that would be wrong. He thinks for a moment, then says: 'It's colder than a penguin's parlour.' The group murmur their appreciation. Cyril says 'It's colder than Leningrad that night the heating went.' The group, as one, go 'Aye'. George says: 'It's cold enough to take your heart and squeeze it into an ice cube.' Cyril: 'As cold as the winter that took our Wilf.' The group, as one, go 'By'. George: 'Cold enough to make a snowman shiver.' There's light applause in the queue, as the clouds get greyer than ever.

There's a pause in the conversation, as though George and Cyril are boxers between rounds. It's certainly getting

colder, and the queue is hopping from foot to foot like birds on ice. The sky is as grey as my hair, and that's saying something.

Cyril clears his throat and the new round begins. 'It's as cold as an icicle down your back,' he says, and everyone shivers, involuntarily. George smiles. He's thought of a good un: 'It's colder than an igloo without a roof,' he says with a flourish and an air of triumph. It could be a winner.

Cyril takes a deep breath to respond, and that could be his big mistake; he fills his lungs full of air which is, to quote his mate George, colder than an igloo without a roof. Cyril turns a deep shade of blue and opens his mouth to speak. The air is almost solid with cold. He says something and a strange thing happens: George and the rest of the Post Office queue watch the words coming out of his mouth in the form of ice bubbles. They hang in the air, suspended like baubles on a Christmas tree. It's so cold that Cyril's words have frozen. George opens his mouth to say something and he finds that his words are frozen, too, hanging there like cold, cold bubbles. Everyone in the queue starts to speak and all their words are icy stalagtites in the air. It's like looking at a cartoon in the paper, like looking at people talking in speech balloons. Except these balloons are frozen. They'd like to move but they can't. They'd like to shout for help but they can't.

Suddenly the door of the Post Office opens and out comes Mrs Wilson with a box of matches. Mrs Wilson has seen it all before; after all, she was the one who had to thaw out the Lord Mayor's Speech in 1963 when it just hung frozen in front of his chain of office. She strikes a match, holds it close to the frozen words, and one by one they melt and we can finally hear Cyril's winning line: 'Colder than the eyes of a polar bear when he's gazing into a snowstorm on Christmas Eve.'

I think that's the winner, don't you?

There's that old saying, favoured by jumper-wearers everywhere as spring pokes its nose round the door, 'Never cast a clout till May is out!' or in other, more local, words, 'Keep thi cardy on till t' summer else tha'll get chilblains like dustbin lids!'. There's another wise saw that's less universally acknowledged but which contains just as much truth, especially for Yorkshire folk: 'In April the vest/Should still protect the chest' and in those few words are contained that huge practical and philosophical dilemma for the average Yorkshireman. It's an old Leyburn phrase that Noel Coward adapted for his little-known musical about the short man whose job was to count all the chickens in Swaledale, 'Brief Hen Counter' (and you've got to imagine this being sung by Noel Coward attempting a Yorkshire accent), 'Vest divesting's never best/it's not in your inter-est/until at least the month you are in/doesn't have a single R in!'. The song was written

for the hero of the musical, Bert Hepplewaite, to sing, and Bert is typical of men from this part of the country in that he doesn't want to take his vest off, even as spring blooms and summer approaches.

Let's take a look at this North Riding street scene. There's a bloke walking to the butcher's in the spring sunshine; he's wearing a bright blue Bri-nylon shirt and underneath you can clearly see his vest. He passes his mate and his mate is wearing a bright green Bri-nylon shirt and underneath you can clearly see his vest as well. They nod to each other smugly as they cross, and the nod seems to say 'I'm not taking my vest off till August, no matter how hot it gets!'. A third man passes; he's wearing a purple Bri-nylon shirt, and underneath he's sporting a string vest that looks like the kind of net you might chuck over the side of a trawler, and the two other vestees give him a thumbs-up of respect. Some people might call this a wonderful diorama, bubbling with a kind of White Rose folksiness; I think it's tragic. I think we Tykes place too much emphasis on the vest.

So here is my personal message to the men of Yorkshire, and let me begin by confessing to something that might startle you: I've not worn a vest since I was a kid, despite the fact that I'm a proud Yorkshireman. I let the vest go with my short trousers and my junior school pumps. I wouldn't be seen dead in a vest unless I was going to a fancy dress party as Bruce Willis in Die Hard 3. Men of Yorkshire, look out of the window: it's April. The Sun is shining. The birds are whistling Ilkley Moor Baht 'At. Men of Yorkshire: take off your vests. Chuck 'em away. Use 'em as dusters. Give 'em to the kids to play with. If you need a white flag, use your vest. If you need a hairnet for somebody with an unusually large head, give them your string vest. Feel the freedom.

If you can't go all the way to start with, then maybe you could just lose the vest for half-an-hour during the hottest part of the day. Perhaps you could un-vest every Tuesday. Maybe you could then invest in off-vesting the vest every other day. Take these small steps and eventually you'll be vestless. And you'll feel better for it, I promise you.

Next month, though, let's make it more difficult. Let's think about losing the cap. That's right. You heard me properly. Losing the cap. Be bold, men of Yorkshire, be bold; you have nothing to lose but those red rings round your foreheads.

Now that it's high summer and the white flat cap is rescued from the back of the wardrobe and the sandals have been matched with the socks and the suncream has been rubbed on the forearms and the back of the chafing neck, I reckon it's time for a number of Yorkshiremen up and down the county to ditch the affectation that stops them enjoying the season to the full.

I'm not referring to the inappropriate wearing of the cardigan on red hot mornings, or the licking of a lolly in the full sun as it melts down the aforementioned cardigan. I'm not on about the way that Yorkshiremen often keep the windows shut even though the house is stifling 'in case the wasps get in' and I'm not referring to the fact that they often insist on having a full roast dinner on a Sunday even

though the temperature is in three figures. Nope, I'm referring to the old collapsed mohican of the Yorkshire gentleman, the dead quiff that tells a lie. I'm referring, of course,
to the combover.

A combover, let's face it, is like a wig or a couple of
home wins at the start of a new football season: nobody is
fooled. Or, perhaps, it fools them for a second, which is
worse. As the comboveree (as we'll call them) walks out
of the house it looks for a tiny stretch of time as though
they've got a full head of hair and then a tiny breeze, a
zephyr, a mini-zephyrette, blows and the combover sprouts

from the head like seaweed from the ocean in a storm. Nervous dogs are frightened and small children cry. 'What's happening to that man's head, Mummy?' 'Shut up and chew your parkin!'

And the Yorkshireman has to go back into his house and sculpt the hair back onto his head with some unguents, creams and sellotape. It's not worth it, boys, it really isn't.

I saw a rare example of a back-combover the other day. Most combovers are from the side, like Arthur Scargill's or Frank Bough's, but just occasionally you get one that begins almost at the top of the spine, almost at the back of the neck. I saw the back-combover in a place that I'll call Kettlewell, because that's where it was.

At first it looked like a small child had been scribbling on a light bulb with a felt tip pen or it looked like some spaghetti had been laid carefully and with no little skill across a balloon. Beneath the 'hair' as I have to refer to it, the Yorkshireman was wearing a frown of deep, deep concentration like Norman Slatterthwaite did just before he invented the wheel in Giggleswick. This man was trying to keep his combover still by sheer willpower.

Tears were trickling from his scrunched-up eyes and his fists were clenched as though he was about to enter a brawl, which in some ways he was: he was in a fight to the death with his recalcitrant hair. It was a warm day and he was perspiring freely. The hair snaked in long, long strands across his skull and the whole edifice looked as delicate as a house of cards. The inevitable happened: a man in leather zoomed by on a motorbike and the breeze from the bike lifted the bloke's hair like a hat. He looked distraught and thrust a flat cap on to his head but the damage had been done and the hair dangled from his cap like bellropes in a cathedral.

So come on, men of Yorkshire. You trust me, don't you? I'm a fellow Yorkshireman. Okay, I've got a full head of hair but I'm just lucky. Make this the summer you chuck over the combover! Make this the July you turn your Yorkshire pate to the sun and shout 'I'm bald and I don't care!'. Buy plenty of suncream, though.

When I think about November in Yorkshire I think about fireworks fizzing up like white roses into the autumn sky and when I think about fireworks I think about Uncle Charlie running into the house to try and hide. He wasn't my real uncle, of course; as far as I can tell nobody was, in those days. He was a tall man who worked down the pit and who, in the Simon Cowell style, wore trousers with the waist somewhere around nipple-height. He wore glasses and collarless shirts and his hobby was photography. As a child I'd spend many hours sitting with him in his darkroom as he developed pictures and his breath laboured in his pit-wrecked chest.

As bonfire day approached me and my mates would become increasingly, almost deliriously, excited, and Uncle Charlie would become more withdrawn, spending longer than usual in his darkroom. 'Don't you like fireworks, Uncle Charlie?' I'd ask, and he'd shake his head. He had a colourful way of describing things: 'Can't stand 'em, kid. Jumping Jacks, Chinese Crackers, Whizzers, Bangers, Whizz Bangers or Helicopters. Can't stand 'em.' Later I looked into my box of Standard Fireworks and I couldn't find any Jumping Jacks or Chinese Crackers but I didn't tell him that.

Uncle Charlie quite liked the bonfire part of Bonfire Night; he liked the way our faces glowed in the flames, he liked the parkin that Mrs Bowley brought from next door, he liked the jacket spuds and he liked the sausages held close to the fire on an old toasting fork, but when the fireworks came out he'd make his excuses and leave.

I'm sorry to confess, that one year me and my mates decided to play a trick on him. We'd wait until he was sitting on a deckchair in the garden, watching the flames and sucking on a triangle of bonfire toffee, and then we'd chuck a jumping cracker that Geoff had found on a dodgy stall on Wombwell Top Market under the chair. We'd see Uncle Charlie dance like Jeff Chandler in Cochise. Cruel,

I know; but these were far-off days before I became the civilised person I am today.

It was a clear, cold Bonfire Night. Memory tells me that it must have been about 1964, when I was eight. The fire was roaring and Mrs Bowley's parkin tasted heavenly. My dad was handing out roast spuds and my brother was wearing a pork pie hat and eating a pork pie, which seemed like a perfect mixture of attire and diet. Uncle Charlie was content, having taken his top set out so that he could suck the toffee harder. Geoff had a glint in his eye. I had a jumping cracker in my pocket. The time approached. Geoff looked at me, nodded, and produced his dad's lighter.

What happened next could be blamed on all sorts of things, but I mainly blame it on the vast, flapping turn-ups on Uncle Charlie's trousers. We chucked the cracker (please don't try this at home) and it jumped and cracked. It landed in Charlie's left turn-up. He leaped in the air. He tried to run. He ended up jumping, like the cracker. The bottom of his trousers caught fire and he hopped across the lawn like Hermes the Winged Messenger of the Gods with his Shoes of Flame, except they were the Turn-ups of Fire.

I'm sorry, Charlie. I'm really sorry. I'm sorry I never said sorry before.

April's here, and we know just what that means: all across Yorkshire barbers and hairdressers are sharpening their scissors ready for what's known as the Spring Rush. Through the winter months the Yorkshireman has let his hair grow. He's become, in the common parlance, a bit wiggy or a little bit overgrown or just this side of

Rapunzel. Now, with the nights drawing out and the evenings getting lighter, it's time for a trim. The barbers are breathing a collective sigh of relief because it's been a harsh winter and although long hair keeps your brain warmer it doesn't put food on the hairdresser's table. They stand at the doors of their salons, smiling. The rush will soon be coming down the street, hair waving in the breeze like seaweed.

The average Yorkshireman can always tell when he needs a haircut after the winter because, let's be honest about this, his flat cap is no longer flat. It's a little off kilter, a bit like the tile in the bathroom that lifted slightly when the old mineworkings under the house shifted. The hair under the cap had built into a bouffant or a super-quiff or what my mother used to call a Busby, named after the hats the Coldstream Guards wore. April is Post-winter Involuntary Cap Lift Month. Time for some drastic scissor action.

Given that Yorkshire people are traditionally thrifty, I'm

surprised that more of us don't cut our own hair. I guess it's the two sides of the Yorkshire coin: we're thrifty, but we like to see a job well done, and we know that if we cut our hair ourselves we'd end up looking like (another of my mother's phrases) alfalfa. So we submit to the buzzing and the snip-snip and, if we're really wanting to smarten ourselves up, the handful of jollop rubbed into the scalp.

Ah yes, the jollop. The cream. The oil. The lard. The grease. The oil. Most Yorkshiremen, me included, don't want anything rubbed into their hair, partly because it reminds us of that childhood incident on the front at Scarborough when that seagull swooped low for Uncle Charlie's dropped chip, and partly because it just seems like too much fuss, too much faff. And anyway, wouldn't it make the cap stick to the head? But when it comes to Great April Shearing Time, you will sometimes find the odd White Rose County denizen who gives a curt nod when the barber holds up the jar of hair gel with an enquiring eyebrow lifted.

And that's because it's spring. 'April is stirring the dull roots', as the great Harrogate poet T S Eliot said, and there's something in the soul of even the scruffiest and tattiest Compo-impersonating Tyke that wants to look a bit more presentable. It's April and it's time to chuck off winter's traces and take a bit of care with your appearance.

So, if you're reading this in Yorkshire, put down the book and wander into the street; you'll see an amazing sight. You'll see flocks of Yorkshiremen with new haircuts. There'll be short-back-and-sides and flat-tops and skinheads and side partings as deep as a moat. There'll be itchy necks and portions of skin that haven't seen the sun since Halloween. There'll a 'tache where there used to be a beard and there'll be an empty and tender face where the sideburns used to dwell. And there will be a whiff in the air; just a hint of one, just a little bouquet. A smell of jollop, of cream, of gel. Not on every head, of course, just the odd one. Just enough to convince you that spring is really here, tha knows.

Listen in at the doors of houses all over Yorkshire as September comes knocking and you'll hear the same phrase echoing like (a) a harbinger of doom, or (b) an angelic chorus promising blessed relief. Of course, the phrase is 'school in the morning!' and after the long and glorious summer break it strikes fear and/or joy into the heart, depending on whether you're a pupil or a harassed parent.

I reckon the idea of school on Monday is particularly challenging if you're a child who's making what they call these days a 'transition'; a transition from infants to juniors, from bottom juniors to top juniors, or of course the huge transition from junior to secondary school.

In the modern world the ground is, quite properly, prepared. Nervous infants have a look at what the big boys and girls do in the mystical land beyond the sand tray and equally nervous top juniors have visits to a place that gradually reveals itself to be friendly and welcoming and not entirely populated by huge adults in school uniform who speak a language from another planet and have faces entirely made of coarse hair.

When I made the leap from junior to secondary in 1967,

though, things weren't like that. I went from the cosy nest of Low Valley Juniors in Darfield to the sprawling megalopolis of Wath Grammar School. They had uniforms. They had a motto. They had houses. They played rugby.

I knew all this because in late July I'd had a letter informing me of the rules. It told me that my parents had to buy a certain number of shirts of a certain colour, trousers of a certain kind, and a white woodwork apron that fastened at the back. Presumably because those front-fastening woodwork aprons might enflame the girls who were busy doing domestic science in back-fastening

pinnies. One important thing the letter pointed out was that this was to be the first year that new boys fresh from junior school didn't have to wear short trousers or caps; I guess it was a grudging acknowledgement that somewhere outside the Yorkshire coalfield the 1960s were happening, but it led to one of the great moments of shared embarrassment and horror that I can remember in all my half-century-plus of life.

I felt good that first morning in my long trousers. My curly hair was cap-free as I trooped into the assembly hall with all the other first-years. We settled down to listen to Miss Clegg, the formidable deputy head, telling us which forms we'd be in. Suddenly, the door opened and a boy walked in. Let's call him Boy X. He, or his parents, hadn't taken in the no shorts/no cap dictum. He looked like he'd stepped from the set of a Just William film. His knees shone in the September sun. His grey socks were pulled up to the correct level and if you looked very carefully you could tell they were held up by elastic garters that you could buy on Barnsley Market in packs of six. His cap was at exactly the right angle on his head, an angle that showed up his new haircut, the one he got for the grammar school in a barber's full of joshing pitmen who said 'Watch out: they'll shove thi heead down t' lavs!'.

Boy X stood transfixed like an office junior who had been misinformed that the company Christmas party was fancy dress. Every first-year pupil turned to look at him at exactly the same moment. We were synchronized turners, participants in a contemporary dance piece called Look At Those Shorts. His face turned tomato red in the stunned silence. He attempted, heartbreakingly, to cover his knees and remove his cap with the same hand. One of his garters snapped with a sound like a starting pistol. I'm sorry I joined in the laughter, Pupil X: I couldn't help it. Just couldn't help it at all.

I'm not sure why, but November time makes me want to reach for rhyme. It seems to stir my poet's blood and bring words rushing in a flood. Some say that spring's a poet's season but I reply that there's no reason November can't be just as fine for making lines that scan and rhyme. I realise that fine and rhyme aren't complete rhymes but give me time: I'm only just getting into gear as my verse stirs now November's here. I realise that didn't scan either but I'm in the grip of a rhyming fever caused by this month's arrival on the scene of November, the month that's a poem machine.

You can keep April, you can keep June: in September I shout 'November soon!'. I tell you, by the end of May I sit and count the slow, slow days till November comes over the horizon with images lovely and weather surprisin'. In the August heat I sit and wait for November to dash from the starting gate. October's the starter but November's the main: I'm gagging for it to be Nov again.

Think of Yorkshire in November; images that you'll remember like fiery sunsets over t' Dales, and morning trails left by snails. Your breath in the air like wreaths of steam, and the bare tree branches like a gorgeous dream. Bonfires glowing like old Jim's nose, halfway between a plum and a rose. Wrapped in scarves and hats and gloves, you do the early morning walk that you've always loved, and the moon hangs there a ten pence piece and you feel fulfilled and you feel at peace.

And I realise that piece and peace are soft rhymes like a llama's fleece but I can't help it: help me please. I've got November rhyme disease. This always happens, every year: my rhymes start off so very clear. As the calendar turns to November 1st my rhymes begin with a crafted burst but as the month drags on and on I find my enthusiasm, and my rhymes are gone and by the time the month has done I'd like to take my rhymes and shoot 'em with a gun.

It's dark and cold and it gets my chest: by the fourth week of the month my rhymes need a rest and my scansion

as feeble as a chocolate kettle which wouldn't work of course since all kettles are made of metal.

Oh dearie me what can I do? I'll have to rhyme till this month's through! I started with such enthusiasm now it's just a little dribble and a rhyming spasm. Yes: November skies as dark as ink, November winds that make you blink, November fireworks with that gunpowder stink, November takes me to the brink of thinking that my rhymes will sink beneath the weight of November fog. Oh, I've been bitten by the rhyming dog. Oh, I've been kissed by the rhyming gran: I'm Mr November, rhyming man. Oh, I've been slapped by the rhyming hand: I'm making rhymes that even I don't understand.

Oh come on, November, hurry up! I need to drain the rhyming cup. I need December to be now then I can stop this dreadful row, these awful rhymes like clunking stones that fall down a ridge to the churchyard bones.

That one's not bad though: keep 'em going. November might be rhyme but in December it'll be snowing. I like November, rhymes and all: November rhymes will never pall. November is the rhyming month: it rhymes …it rhymes …what rhymes with month?

Now, as we know, all Yorkshire folk love to get summat for nowt; that's why I often bump into lamp posts because I'm walking with my head down looking for discarded change on the pavement, and why I always like the pie that I got free more than the one I paid for in the 'Buy One Get One Free' promotion. And it's doubly delicious if you pay for the Buy One Get One Free with the

money you found on the floor. Result! So we should all be delirious with joy this month because it's February in a Leap Year and so we get an extra day for nothing. And for this reason I think that the Leap Day must have been invented by a Yorkshireman, fiddling about with a calendar one cold February evening in the Dark Ages. That's the Dark Ages Arms near Pickering. Suddenly, he looked up and said: 'Ah've fahnd a day hiding round t' back of t' page!' and the leap year was born.

Yes, 29th February is a bonus, a free 24 hours when we can do what we like and, if we play our cards right, it won't count towards our eventual total, the Three Score and Ten that we're meant to end up with. It's like a private public holiday, a day free from the normal bounds of convention and polite society. It's a leap day in the leap year so I can do what the heck I like.

The question is, what? What can I do to highlight this extra day, and, more to the point, what kind of Yorkshire related thing can I do to celebrate the day? After all, if you get an extra day for nothing and the day was invented by a Yorkshireman, then you may as well fill it with Tyke-related things that won't ever come back to haunt you because this is a day like no other. The usual shackles that stop you doing ridiculously Yorkshire-centric things have been shattered and at the end of the day they'll mend themselves and they won't be shattered again for another four years. So get cracking.

Here goes: I'll go for a fifteen-mile hike across the Dales in the gnashing February wind wearing only a flat cap and a smile. I'll make a Yorkshire pudding as big as a trampoline and spend all day eating it and the gravy will flood down at least two of my chins and I won't care. I'll go down to London on the train and talk to everybody in the broadest Yorkshire accent I can muster, tha knows, and I won't care if they can't understand a word I say. I'll go for a twenty-mile hike across the moors wearing only a muffler and a grin. I'll stand up in a library and sing all the verses of Ilkley Moor Baht 'At and at the same time I'll act it out with silhouettes and glove puppets and performing whippets in authentic costume. I'll go into a shop to buy something and enquire about the price and then shout 'HOW MUCH?' and leave the shop without paying for the item or picking it up. I'll rush into the Olympic Stadium and start playing knurr and spell until the security guards tell me to stop, and then I'll teach them the game and then we'll all get chucked out and we just won't mind one little bit. I'll eat a piece of parkin so huge that it can be seen by the pilots of passing aircraft. I'll spend the entire day just saying EEE and BY and AYE and NAY. I'll go for a thirty-mile hike down the coast wearing only a pair of pit socks and a thoughtful pout.

These are just my ideas, of course: I'm sure you can think of more daft Yorky things to do to highlight this golden day. Come on, let's go: it's summat for nowt!

May, as all us early risers know, is the perfect time of year for the dawn chorus; as May progresses towards June the chorus gets earlier and earlier and louder and more strident until it seems like the first bird is

beginning to sing just a few moments after your head has touched the pillow and you're drifting to the land of zizz.

For the last couple of years, though, I've noticed a very interesting phenomenon, and I don't know if it's confined to my corner of Yorkshire or if it's a county-wide thing but I think it's a significant change in bird behaviour. Put simply, in our garden the dawn chorus is happening in Yorkshire dialect. If you don't believe me, let me describe to you a recording I made of the birdsounds the other night just before dawn. The tape begins with silence, the delicious silence of the middle of the night. Actually, it isn't completely silent: there's a car moving slowly down the main road to Doncaster and you can hear somebody in a house sneezing. Then you hear me fiddling with the recording device and asking myself 'Is it on? Is this thing on? One, two, one, two …oh it must be on'. And then there's silence again.

Then the first bird begins. A single noise, sounding just like an aged Yorkshireman climbing up a steep incline: 'By …'. For a while, this is the only sound we hear, repeated at regular intervals from somewhere deep within the hedge. 'By ….'. Pause. 'By ….'. Pause.

Then the 'By …' is joined by a faster, more rhythmic call from a little bird in a little tree: 'By Heck By Heck By Heck' it goes, and it overlays the 'By …' like a jazz band setting up a groove. Then a deeper note can be heard, from a bigger bird high up in the branches of one of the old trees in the cemetery at the back of our house. 'Happen!' it says, and then again 'Happen!' and every so often 'Happen So!'.

And the dawn chorus builds like a Yorkshire Symphony. On top of the 'By …' and the 'By Heck By Heck By Heck' and the deep bass 'Happen ...' there's a busy bird whistling 'I'll tell thi summat tha knows' over and over again like a bore at a bus stop and there's a lonely off-key couple of notes that sound like 'Eyup! Eyup! Eyup!' over and over again as a bird on the bird-bath responds to the pull of spring by calling for a mate in the only way Yorkshire creatures know. And could that be a female of the species answering from the birdbath in next door's garden: 'Now then! Now then! Now then!'? I think it could.

Some kind of finch is warbling 'I'm mixing mi puddins I'm mixin mi puddins!' and there's a bird of prey high in the air shouting 'I'm brussen! I'm brussen!' and it certainly is. Two birds are squabbling over a dropped crisp, both uttering a couple of sounds that could, to the trained Yorkshire ear, be 'Geeor!' and 'Geeor nar!'.

The tape fills up as the Yorkshire dawn chorus builds and builds into a monumental wall of sound. I wonder if I've stumbled on something unique here, or would a Scottish McDawn chorus include tweets that sounded like 'Och aye!' and single notes that sounded like 'Jings!', and would an American dawn chorus begin with lonely males chirruping 'Howdy pardner!' and lonely females replying 'Hi Honey! Hi Honey! Hi Honey?' Nobody really knows.

And does the Tyke dawn chorus sound like it's in broad Yorkshire because I'm broad Yorkshire myself and I've transferred my own language onto our feathered friends? Again, who knows? The tape's stopped now, and I'm feeling tired because I've been up so long, but I know that I'll be back again in the morning for t' dawn chorus, waiting for that first 'By ...' to echo through the half-darkness.

Well, it's that time of year again; it's the moment to reveal this year's Most Used Summer Phrases in Yorkshire. I hope you're excited: I certainly am. I hope it's a nail-biter like last year's was, when it was a close-run thing between 'You're not going to the shops in them flip-flops!' and 'Plain crisps really are a vegetarian option, mam!'. In the end, the plain crisps won after a recount. And that's the first time I've ever typed that particular sentence.

Each year from June to August a team of Yorkshire Listening Volunteers sit in cafés, pubs, at bus stops, on railway platforms, on the buses and the trains, and simply anywhere in Yorkshire where people gather for pleasure and write down the phrases used by the general public.

These phrases are then fed by hand into a powerful and

ecologically friendly (it's fuelled by sheep droppings) computer and the result is published in the *Dalesman* magazine in October. I know that linguists take great note of our findings, and new editions of dictionaries are often meatier and more interesting as a result of the work of our DLVs, so flat caps off to them.

Anyway, here are the top four Most Used Summer Phrases, in reverse order. At number four there's that old favourite 'I think it's clearing up', often said with an artificially bright grin to a group of kids behind a sodden windbreak on a beach. This summer has been particularly damp and so we've heard the phrase more often than we normally would. Indeed, after hot summers the phrase almost becomes extinct, but it's one of those organisms that remains dormant until circumstances bring it back to life, like the Eyeless Toad of Muker. One of our volunteers reported hearing the phrase fifteen times on one morning of rain, hail and thunder, along with its variations 'There's a touch of blue sky over the chip shop' and 'whose idea was it to leave the anoraks in the B&B?'.

At number three there was a new phrase, bespoke for the Olympics: 'Who knocked Grandma's ornaments off last night doing the Usain Bolt celebration?'. As usual with phrases like this there were variations like 'Who scared Grandma's parrot/Who put Grandma off her online Bingo/who poked Grandma in the eye … doing the Usain Bolt Celebration?'.

At number two, a phrase that keeps popping up over the years, uttered with various shades of irony and endless layers of meaning: 'Why go abroad?'. Again, this is often heard on freezing cold promenades or during exhaustion stops on cycling holidays. Our Listening Volunteers heard it uttered in moorland pubs as the rain pounded the windows in almost biblical fashion, in the queue at an ice-cream van near a Yorkshire beauty spot that you couldn't see because of the drizzle, and being shouted from the passenger seat of a car to a harassed dad trying to change a tyre in a lay-by. Of course, whoever says it is being sarcastic on an industrial scale. Of course, that's part of the fun.

And (drum roll) the winner of this year's Most Used Summer Phrase in Yorkshire is: 'I told you not to touch the side of the tent!'. A worthy winner, I think you'll agree. We've all been there, in the quagmire of a campsite with the family playing Scrabble in a deluge when one of the kids, accidentally or not, leans over and touches the side of the tent. Water leaks in. Water seeps in. You may as well be outside. Anger rises. Voices are loud. Scrabble tiles are arranged into words that can't be repeated in a family book.

The 'I Told You Not To Touch The Side Of The Tent' T-shirts, pinnies and umbrellas will be in the shops in plenty of time for Christmas, and I'm getting excited for next year already, aren't you?

As it's the start of a new year, a time when we all turn over a fresh leaf and look forward to the year ahead with excitement rather than trepidation, I thought I'd share my New Year's Resolutions with you, and then we'll check on December 31st and see how many I've stuck to.

I resolve to mention Yorkshire at all times, even when the word is inappropriate in a sentence. So, for example,

if somebody asks me what the time is, I'll reply 'It's ten to three in Yorkshire!' even if I'm in Kuala Lumpur or Barbed Wire, Michigan. If somebody asks me the answer to a simple sum, for example two plus two, I'll reply 'Four, in Yorkshire numbers!'. I realise this may get irritating for listeners, especially those from other, less favoured, counties.

I resolve to wear the Yorkshire uniform of flat cap and muffler at all times, even in extreme heat. I also resolve, by means of the serious look on my face and the disingenuous set of my jaw, to give the impression that I'm not wearing them ironically in the manner of a student at a fancy dress party. I resolve to begin every meal, even breakfast and high tea in posh cafés, with a Yorkshire pudding. If I'm eating out I will take the Yorkshire pudding mix with me in a plastic tub and ask the café to make me a pudding. If they refuse I resolve to take my custom elsewhere. And my gravy.

I resolve to visit at least one lesser county (Lancashire, perhaps, or Avon) each month and try to persuade the denizens of said county that Yorkshire is superior in every way. I resolve to make trays of curd tart and parkin to give out to the denizens who will then be convinced that Yorkshire is the best county, especially if my parkin is as good as it normally is, and not soggy and brittle at the same time as it was when I made it last Tuesday when I had a heavy cold. Sorry. No excuses: I'm a Yorkshireman! Which leads me on to my next resolution …

I resolve never to apologise or make excuses, which will of course mark me out as a true cast-iron gold-standard Yorkshireman. If I spill tea on the best tablecloth I will blame the cup handle, and if that fails I will blame the tablecloth for being in the wrong place at the wrong time. If my Yorkshire puddings turn out soggy I won't make excuses; I'll blame myself and I'll say it's because I once visited Oxfordshire, where all Yorkshire puddings are as soggy as a patch of damp on an outhouse wall.

I resolve to sing Ilkley Moor Baht 'At, loudly and out of tune, at least once a day in settings as diverse and inappropriate as the library and a village cricket match. If people object on the grounds of taste or decency I will simply sing the song in a louder voice, as all Yorkshiremen should.

I resolve to only go shopping and on holiday within the bounds of Yorkshire. If I find that a beach or beauty spot sneaks into another county I will steer well clear of the, say

Lincolnshire, side of the attraction in case I stumble into it accidentally and somehow become contaminated with YellowBellyness. I resolve that any further children I have (unlikely, I know) will be called variations on the word Yorkshire. York for a boy, or Yorky, or Yorkness. Yorka for a girl, or Yorkee or Yorkina. If they wish to change their names to Yorkshire or Mr or Mrs Yorkshire Yorkshire, I resolve never to stand in their way.

And finally, I resolve to allus speyk in t' strongest Yorksher dialect that ah can, just to confuse t' others, tha knows.

Halloween has more or less been completely taken over by Trick or Treat, an American invention that involves pre-teens in masks knocking on your door demanding money, like junior muggers. Mind you, a mate of mine said 'Trick, please' to a lad dressed as Bela Lugosi's Dracula and was amazed when the boy pulled three rabbits and a trout out of his hat. That's my mate's hat, not the lad's. He got to keep the trout because the lad didn't know it was there.

Older readers will, of course, recall the Yorkshire equivalent of Trick or Treat, Gizzit, which flourished in the north and west of the county between the wars. The tradition was that the young people of the village would gather at a known landmark, the market cross, say, or a park bench, in the early evening of Halloween, and chant the ancient Gizzit Evocation: 'Gizzit, Gizzit, Gizziteer, Giz thi brass for cakes and beer! Gizzit, Gizzit, Gizzit Nar or I'll go to yer washing line and steal yer mam's best bra!'. Those same older readers have told me it was the saying

of the word 'bra' that caused most excitement and that indeed they'd chant it as many times as they could until younger people in the group had to be hosed down or sent home or both.

The group would then march around the village knocking on doors and refusing to go away until brass had been dropped into the 'brass bag'. Anybody not giving brass would be subjected to the violent Gizzit Bumps, an odd practice which involved tossing the skinflints in the air from the Gizzit Blanket and sometimes dropping them on the floor. Very few people, of course, refused to pay up and those that did only had one or two sessions of Gizzit

Bumps before they delved deeply into their purses. Apart from Tight Trevor of Tingley, but he's worth a book all on his own.

Some say that 1938, that odd and stifling autumn towards the end of the decade, was the high point of Gizzit. Adults began to join in the fun, and visitors from all over the country thronged to the places where the Gizzit marching began. It could be said, as we hinted at earlier, that this was one of the few times in the 1930s that you could actually say the word bra in public to somebody who wasn't your mother and who you weren't married to, or at least engaged to. Teams of doctors and nurses were often on standby to treat the overheating known as Bra Shout Blush which was known to affect up to five per cent of the Gizziteers.

Contemporary photographs show hundreds of people marching to empty houses carrying huge Gizzit Sacks in those pre-war years. The houses are deserted because everyone in the village is actually in the parade, thus almost rendering the commercial basis of Gizzit useless. Local composers created tunes for brass bands and choirs to perform, the most famous of which is probably Bertram's Gizzit Variations, which culminates with the entire choir (and anybody else who might be passing) shouting 'Bra!' at the tops of their voices.

Most people agree that it was the coming of the Second World War that led to the demise of Gizzit as a local tradition. The blackout meant that it was hard to walk through darkened streets without stubbing your toes or dropping your Gizzit Bag. Many of the marchers and most of the doctors and nurses were away fighting, and the shouting of 'Bra!' may have alerted enemy troops to the presence of a washing line they could have used to tie you up with.

Gizzit hung on in a few places up to the early 1950s; the last known instance of it being in the Dales in 1952, when a mere handful of people trudged through the streets simply because they thought they should, at which point it's always time for a tradition to curl up and die. Although, I'm thinking of reviving it. Any takers? You get to shout interesting words in public.

There's a moral to this story and the moral is: You Never Learn. Or, to be more precise: I Never Learn. When I was a young boy growing up in South Yorkshire in the 1960s April Fool's Day was a Big Thing. If you can imagine how big Halloween is these days, that's how big April Fool's Day was then. All the comics I read would be full of it, and TV programmes would get you to do things like put a slice of bread on top of the telly because they were sending out rays that would toast it, and newspapers would carry reports about things like Chocolate Mines and Hidden Tunnels that connected Buckingham Palace to a chip shop in Otley. I believed both of those, of course: I left a slice of Mother's Pride on the television until it went green and I begged my parents to take me tunnel-hunting in Otley.

All this media attention meant that I was as excited as anyone about it and I began to plan my epic April Fool jokes way back in January, when April was a distant photo of a barn in the Dales on our calendar in the back room.

So, one year I typed out a note in capital letters on a bit of scrap paper. It said PAY US THE MONEY YOU OWE US OR WE'LL SEND THE BOYS ROUND. I folded the note until it was the same size as a stamp and put it through the letterbox of the old gent who lived nearby and who sold the local sporting paper, the *Green Un*, on street corners on a Saturday afternoon. I imagined that he would read the note, be momentarily jolted by it, and then realise it was an April Fool gag.

Of course, the opposite happened. He read the note and

was scared to death by it. He ran next door to show his neighbour, in a state of some agitation. His neighbour had seen me sneaking off and put two and two together. They came round to our house with the offending bit of paper. When they showed it to my mam and dad it didn't seem funny at all. It seemed absurd, and stupid, and vindictive. My excuse that it was an April Fool joke didn't wash, and I was roundly told off and I had to apologise to the old gent. I wept and asked him if he'd got a hanky. 'Any colour will do,' I said. 'A white one or a red one. Mind you, a *Green Un* would be best.' I ducked as my mam aimed a clip at my ear.

You'd think this would have put me off April Fool jokes but, as I said, I never learn. So the next year, inspired by something I'd seen in the *Beano*, I painted some pebbles yellow and, late in the evening of March 31st, buried them in our front garden and then, early the next day, dug them up and put them on a table near the gate next to a shakily-written sign that said GOLD NUGETS FOUND IN DARFIELD GARDEN. I didn't realise that I'd spelled nuggets wrong because, after all, I was a prospector not an academic. The old chap who sold the *Green Un* went past and I waved to him and said, 'Come and have a look at these: they're Gold Uns.' If my mam hadn't been hanging the washing out, she'd have given me a clip.

Then some Big Lads from the Top Street came round. 'We've heard tha's found some gold,' one of them said. I went bright red and my voice began to shake. 'Well, I'm only reckoning, like,' I said. 'Let's have a look,' another big lad said, in a voice like a cement mixer. I passed him a pebble. 'These aren't nuggets,' he growled. 'They're pebbles painted yellow.' 'April Fool!' I piped, feebly. I noticed he'd got yellow paint on his huge hands. I never learn.

These days, round the streets and avenues of Yorkshire, Halloween is a big thing and Trick or Treat, judging by the number of kids knocking on your door wearing witches' hats, carrying plastic broomsticks and demanding dosh like miniature Goth debt collectors, is an even bigger thing. I remember, though, when Halloween was hardly celebrated at all round these parts and I vividly recall the time in the late 1960s that me and my mates decided it was time it was. We were avid fans of American TV programmes and we must have seen some freckle-faced, dungaree-wearing kids on I Love Lucy or Mr Ed or Bewitched going through an elaborate Trick or Treat ritual and ending up with some spice (or as they called it, candy) and some belm (or as they called it, moolah).

We weren't completely sure how the whole thing worked, however, because our TVs were old and black-and-white and sometimes the horizontal hold went and sometimes they just conked out altogether and sat there staring back at us sitting there staring at them, and Mr Parry would have to be sent for, and he'd gaze at the telly and tut and say 'Who sold you this?' and we'd remind him it was him and he'd laugh and take it away in his van.

Anyway, me and the Lads gleaned a few facts about what to do: we knew we had to dress up in scary ways, we knew we had to knock on a door and say a rhyme that went something like 'Trick or treat, smell my feet, give us something good to eat'; then the householders would give us cash or sweeties, which became the treat, and if they didn't we'd smash their greenhouse up with sledge-hammers, which became the trick. Don't worry, gentle readers, I would never smash anybody's greenhouse up with a sledgehammer. I'd use a dried-hard Yorkshire pudding. I'm kidding.

So, that Halloween, we all got dressed up in a fairly desultory fashion; one of us wore a black balaclava, one of us had smeared his mam's lipstick on his face to look like blood, one of us wore a colander on his head for reasons that were never quite made clear although it was cleverly fastened on with an elastic band, and one of us had made jagged false fangs from cardboard. We looked like a ram-raid at the tail-end of a jumble sale. I decided we

needed to be more theatrical, and I'd recently acquired some bongo drums from somebody's auntie who'd heard that I wanted to be in a band. 'He can practise on these,' she'd said. 'He can't!' my mam replied. I reckoned that giving it some Latin vibes on the bongos just before we knocked on the door would lend the whole event a touch of class and sophistication. The Lads reluctantly agreed, with nodding colanders and balaclavas.

We approached a darkened house in the middle of the village at random and walked down the path to the front door. If anybody had seen us their overriding emotion would have been pity rather than fear; we looked homeless. Or gormless. We stood nervously in the gloom and I began to pound what I mistakenly thought was a bossanova beat on the bongos; it sounded like somebody falling downstairs in a padded suit. A light went on in the house so I increased the speed and intensity of the rhythm and the Lads began to chant our Trick or Treat ditty. It was like the early days of Hip Hop in The Bronx. Nothing was happening inside the house so I played louder and they chanted faster.

The door flung open to reveal a sight that was much scarier than any Halloween get-up. A skeletal toothless man in paisley pyjamas with his hair sticking out Einstein-fashion shouted 'Will yer shurrup wi' that row? Am on mornins at pit!' and slammed the door deafeningly. We turned and ran, and a colander fell off a terrified head and rolled along the floor. Bongos for sale. Hardly used. One careless owner. Trick or treat?

Right, gentlemen of Yorkshire, do you know what month it is? Yes, that's right: November, the month of accelerating Christmas Present Panic. Now, I know that a number of you will be saying that you don't even think of getting your loved ones a Yuletide gift until the shops have almost shut on Christmas Eve, and that may be true for those of you who know exactly what you're going to buy, but what about the vast majority of Yorkshiremen who have no idea what to buy their wives and who spend the whole of this month trying to wheedle out of their spouses some hint or tip or nod or wink as to what they might want so that they can spend the whole of December trying to find it? The whole humiliating ritual goes something like this …

First three days of November: husband approaches wife, nonchalantly whistling as though he hasn't a care in the world. Husband speaks: 'Would you like a cuppa?' Wife: 'Yes, please.' Husband: 'Er …have you had a think what you might like for Christmas yet?' Wife: It's only the start of November. I've got far too many things to think about before then!' Husband retreats, wounded.

Next three days of November: husband tries to discern, through his wife's reaction to TV adverts, what she might like for Christmas. Husband: 'Do you like that coat? It looks nice on her.' Wife: 'I don't think it would suit me at all. I'd never wear anything like that. How long have we been married? Surely you'd know I'd never wear anything like that!' Husband, abashed: 'Yes, I know. I was only joking.' Wife: 'I like those shoes.' Husband, desperate and grateful: 'Would you like some for Christmas?' Wife: 'Don't be daft. I just said I liked them. I didn't say I wanted any.'

Next three days of November: husband attempts the direct approach. Husband: 'What would you like for Christmas?' Wife: 'I don't know.' Husband: 'Oh, surely you must have some idea what you'd like.' Wife, striking terror into her husband's heart: 'I'll tell you what: surprise me.' Husband goes into the kitchen and gazes into the garden. The S word was the last word he wanted to hear. He remembers the year he got her the ceramic triceratops. Well, it was certainly a surprise.

Next three days of November: husband in a whirl of possible surprises and definitions of the word 'surprise'. Did she really mean 'surprise'? Did she mean 'mild surprise'? Did she mean 'severe surprise'? Did she mean 'shock'? Who knew there were so many gradations of that word? And what counts as a surprise, given his experience with the ceramic triceratops? A cardigan? A kettle? A wheelbarrow? A jigsaw? A pet fish? Flute lessons? A balloon ride? A weekend in Scarborough? A jam-making kit? A map book? A visit to a spa for a special Bingley-method ankle massage? A wood-carving of Dickie Bird? A bottle of wine with her name on the label? A tricycle? The husband is anxious and sweaty. His wife remarks upon this.

Next three days of November: the husband tells the wife what he'd like for Christmas in the hope it might get her to reciprocate. Husband: 'I know what I'd like for Christmas, a nice woolly hat to wear when I go for my walks.' Wife: 'Thanks for that. I'll get you one.' Husband: 'What would you like, then?' Wife: 'I've told you. A surprise.' Husband: 'Maybe I could get you a matching woolly hat like the one you're going to get me'. Wife: 'Ah, then it wouldn't be a surprise, would it?' Husband: 'No, it would be a woolly hat.' Wife: 'Ha. Ha.'

Next three days of November: husband rings round wife's friends to try and ascertain what she might consider a surprise present. The only consensus is that it doesn't matter what it is, as long as it's not another ceramic triceratops.

Next three days of November: husband begins to formulate a plan that the rest of us can see is seriously flawed. Maybe it was just the fact it was a triceratops that his wife didn't like. Maybe another ceramic dinosaur would be the perfect surprise.

Next three days of November: husband buys and takes delivery of a ceramic mammoth. Now that will be a surprise!

Here's a Yorkshire February Legend, in the key of F: It's fiction, of course, but it's a funny finny flowing fitting fiction for February.

February flummoxes even the feistiest of florid Yorkshire farmers: fact. Freezing until frozen, water forms fantastic fantasy swirls and fabulous frosty formations. Fighting through fields full of fallen and falling snow fifteen feet deep, fridge-like, the farmer finds a furry feral fox making faintly feeble sounds with a shuffle and kerfuffle and a sniffle and a snuffle. The February Fox. The February Fox is a famous sign of a fine summer to come. A summer of fun and frolic from Fazakerley to Fartown,

Now there's a couple just made for February

from Froggatt Edge to Featherstone. A summer when Uncle Frank finally asks Freda to be more than his friend, more than his friendly friend, and she falls for him and he faints. A summer of fierce and fiery sun leading to fierce and fiery shoulders and arms, fetlocks and foreheads. A summer when a fully-pumped football flies forward forcefully on the beach, kicked by flabby Francois and flattening little Fred in his functional Fedora who flops then flaps then forces himself to his feet and forgives. No flareup: fortunate. No fighting: fortunate. A forgettable summer? No, an unforgettable summer.

The February Fox must first be fed, though, according to the legend, and then finally the spring will come and fortuitously lead the summer along with fizzing flighty fol-de-rols. And what does the February fox like to eat? Fish. With a fish fork. Not any fish but a fit (not fat) flounder with flapping fins fished in a fine-holed fishnet from the foaming water at Flamborough.

Firm flounder flesh flambéed over a flickering fire and eaten with French fries, flageolet beans, figs, fennel, fudge, fruit and flaming filberts. Only when he's full will the February Fox finally say that spring can come and bring fulfilling summer along with it.

So the farmer flogs fifty-four Fresians to buy the food for the finicky February Fox. Why won't the February Fox have chips? Why does it have to be French Fries? Why can't the February Fox have smouldering nuts? Why does it have to be flaming filberts? Can't it just be Flounder Flavoured Flakes? Does it have to be Flounder flesh? Won't fish fingers fulfil the farmer's part of the bargain? The February

Fox smiles a fetching smile, flicks and flips the flinching family of fleas from his foot-long tail and says 'fetch, farm-boy. Find, farmboy', and the farmer finally goes in search of the fodder, far and further, through the Fjords, through France, through Finland and the Faeroes, and Fiji and the Falklands. Far and further, further and far.

After a quest as long as a folk song, the farmer finds the food and fetches it foxwards. It's all there: The flounder, the French fries, the flageolet beans, the fennel, the fudge, the flaming filberts and the fruit. The farmer forces a fleeting smile. He's even forged and fashioned a fish fork from a Ford Focus fender he found in a forest. The February Fox folds his fickle foxy arms and says, 'Figs? No Figs? No figs feature here!' The farmer feels forlorn and foolish. Feels fig-lack. Feels failure. Fights flaky fury and frissons of funereal frowns after his foray.

The farmer feels responsible. No unforgettable spring, now. No unforgettable summer. Fail. Epic fail. Suddenly something flashes in the sky: The February Fairy from Filey. The February Fairy festooned with fistfuls of figs of all forms and flavours! The February Fairy flings the figs at the Farmer who in his turn flings the figs to the February Fox. Fame for the farmer! Figs (and all the other stuff beginning with F) for the February Fox!

Finish here, folks. February's here, folks. Soon be spring and summer, thanks to the feisty farmer, folks.

Watch it! Careful now! I'm slipping and slairing and sliding down the street like Torvill and/or Dean on an icy February Yorkshire morning. McMillan's Bolero.

...mornin' slippy out int it..

McMillan's BolerOh My Goodness I'm going over. No, I'm not. Managed to save myself by grabbing onto this frosty fence which is cold on my gloveless hands. I don't want to fall, or to be more accurate, I don't want to have a fall. I've noticed that when you're young you fall and when you're older you 'have a fall', like you might have a slice of toast or a haircut. Well, I'm not going down; I'm not going to, in the Barnsley phrase, tummle ovver. I hope.

The Slippy Yorkshire Street: it's like a board game of the sort that families play in the winter. Shake a six to start.

Move along the board, carefully, gingerly. Land on a frozen puddle: go back to the beginning. Shake a double and sail along confidently but then land on a square that represents a slab of black ice and go over like a ton of middle-aged bricks.

Nobody ever gets to the end of the game; you either keep rolling back to the start or you just sit there looking up and gathering the mental and physical strength to shout for assistance from a passer-by, which isn't the sort of strength you normally need when you're playing a board game, let's face it.

I'm moving very slowly down the street now, almost in slow motion, almost coming to a halt. What if I do fall over and break something and find that I can't get up? I'll be like that bloke I once saw in the road one winter's day between the Community Centre and Dent's Shop. He had had a failure of the legs to do what they're supposed to do on the tin and had kissed the pavement. He didn't appear to be hurt but he couldn't get back up even though he bicycled his legs like an upside-down beetle in a sink. People in a similar situation in any other part of the country would shout 'Help!' but because this gentleman was as Yorkshire as they come he was shouting 'Heyop!' which sounds a bit like help but doesn't have a pleading or wheedling edge. Eventually a number of us gathered round and lifted him up and, as we hauled him horizontal, because he was from Yorkshire he tried to pretend that he hadn't fallen over and carried on pointing out some racing pigeons with his stick as they wheeled across the sky.

As we helped him to his slippered feet we rescuers began

to experience that phenomenon known as Group Gravity where a number of the more ungainly amongst us began to tumble and grabbed onto the others who then grabbed onto the fallen man's stick. We looked like a special Morris Dance to herald the hope of the coming of spring or some people who had been eating too many bananas and had thrown down the skins. After a while, once we'd got him perpendicular, we all went our separate ways, which meant that we all fell down separately on our way home with nobody to help us up.

I'm walking really slowly, now. I'm being overtaken by a parked car. I've got to get to the postbox with this birthday card; it's not far to the postbox but it's taking ages. My breath hangs before me in coils, dissipating gradually and making coil oils, as they call them round here. I'm almost there: the postbox is looming into view, glowing like a robin on a branch. Then the long melancholy slide begins. I feel the world rushing past me as though I am on a train. My feet perform a series of movements that are part tap-dance, part cartoon character's on-the-spot running. I try my best not to fall on this crisp winter morning. I flap the card I am going to post as though it might help my balance. A car trundles by and the driver, a man I know, waves at me. Instinctively, I wave back and that proves to be my undoing.

I slip. I flail. I totter. I stagger. I try my very best to defy physics but in the end I fail and I fall. No, I'm 60: I have a fall. I hit the ground and the ground hits me back. I lie there like a body chalked on the floor in a murder mystery film.

I'll have to shout for help. Heyop! Heyop!

Ah, is there anything better than spring in Yorkshire? Anything more wonderful than the March sun peeping from behind the fluffy clouds and warming your face as you walk up the hill? Answer to both rhetorical questions: no. The hill called to me this bright morning, asked me to take a lovely stroll up its gentle slopes and I answered with a resounding 'Aye!'.

Up the hill I go, the sun shining on my smile and reflecting off my glasses with a friendly wink. It's a bit breezy, though, I've got to admit, but you have to expect that in March. Up I go, my heart pumping and doing me good. As long as it doesn't stop pumping I'll be okay. Getting a bit out of breath now; still, they say that's good for you too, although not if you're sitting on the settee. Come on, legs, keep going! Come on heart, keep pounding! It's spring and I'm feeling good!

131

By, it's windy though! I can hardly hear myself think. It's a spring wind of course, not a winter wind, but my eyes are still watering like Malham Tarn. Up we go. Up the hill. Up. The. Hill. Breath coming in short gasps now. Doing. Me. Good. The wind's getting stronger. March wind, blow! Blow, wind and crack your cheeks, as King Theer, the Yorkshire equivalent of King Lear, should have said.

And there goes my cap. Flipping heck, there goes my best flat cap, the one I got for Christmas, caught by the wind and frisbeeing across the hill like a Yorkshire pudding. Good job there are no clay-pigeon shooters nearby or they'd have blasted it to smithereens. There it is, just a bit down the hill, caught in that bush. I'll clamber down and get it. Funny how it sometimes seems steeper going down than going up. My calves are on fire! Mind you, it's doing me good in the March sun. I'll keep telling myself that. Doing me good.

This bush is taller than it looked when I powered past it. It's more of a sapling, almost a tree. And there's my cap, up near the top, wind buffeting the branches as though the tree was the mast of a ship at sea. I reach up, stretching. The cap waves at me with genial contempt. The wind is getting stronger, flapping my scarf like a windsock at an airport. I can't quite reach it, no matter how hard I try, no matter how far I stretch; I came out for a March stroll, not a workout.

There's a stick on the floor, I grab it and start to try to knock the cap out of the bush/sapling/tree. I look a bit like somebody who has lost an argument with nature and I'm punishing it. I'm giving the greenery six of the best, I'm giving it forty lashes. The cap isn't moving. The branch seems to be wearing the cap, seems to be comfortable with the cap. The wind almost blows the cap out of the tree. Almost, but not quite. I'll have to jump. I'll have to jump in the strong March breeze and the shining March sun and wave my discarded stick. I hope nobody's coming.

I hope there are no fellow-strollers around to see the middle-aged man with the silver quiff bouncing up and down as though he's on a trampoline, waving a stick like he's conducting a band. I'll count to three and then I'll jump. Well, maybe I'll count to five. Go on, do it! Jump now! Wave the stick! Shout at the cap because that makes you feel better. Shout at the tree because that makes you feel better. Jump! Wave! Shout! Jump! Wave! Shout!

Of course, this is the moment the walking club come round the corner. 'Morning all. Yes, lovely morning. Yes, just having a little light exercise. Yes, this March wind really gets you going.'

They've gone. Jump! Wave! Shout!

You know it's going to happen; you just know it's going to happen and somehow it should be prevented. It must not happen. I'm referring to the fact that some well-meaning person in a Yorkshire village not far from here will, for the best of all possible intentions, suggest to the school staff or the village hall committee or the group of friends in the pub that this should be the year that they revive the old tradition of dancing round the maypole on the village green on May Day. 'After all, the pole's still there, a bit rusty and a bit battered but it's still there',

they'll say, their eyes gleaming with naive enthusiasm. There will be a murmuring in the room that suggests a kind of muted interest.

The oldest person in the room will tell the rest of the gathering that she remembers dancing round the Maypole before the war with her classmates and then during the war with the refugee children. The interest will become less muted and will begin to gather momentum. A spirit of enterprise will be in the air, fluttering around the room. A newcomer to the village, possibly a graphic designer who is full of fancy city ways, will suggest that they form a Mayday Maypole sub-committee to look into the possibility and, after a silence and another couple of anecdotes from the oldest person in the room, it is agreed (in the strange language of these occasions) that a sub-committee should be formed. Let me repeat my warning: this should not happen. Okay then, take no notice.

As winter gives way to spring plans for the May Day Maypole Dancing are in full swing. Somehow it has become a festival. The WI have gladly agreed to make the ribbons that will be dangled from the pole; children from the village school are practising the dances using pieces of string hung from the hall ceiling. A local folk singer is composing special music that will, he promises, sound traditional. The brass band is coming and there will be stalls and an ice-cream van and face painting. A local minor celebrity who once appeared in Emmerdale will be asked to open the event and he will agree, forgetting that he has double-booked the day with a talk on a Baltic Cruise. It's not too late to give up and abandon the project. It really isn't.

People who know me will know that normally I'm jolly and optimistic and they'll be asking why I've got such a downer, as the young people say, on the idea of the Mayday Maypole dancing. Well, let me explain. Picture the village, the delicate social and cultural make-up of the village, as being a lot like the ribbons of a Maypole. If the ribbons get tangled up then the dance will grind to a halt or, worse, people might bump into each other and Maypole-based injuries will occur. In the same way, if a disparate group of people, specifically Yorkshire people, are brought together to complete a community-based task then, metaphorically, their ribbons will get tangled. There will be discussions about the music.

The discussions will heat up gently. They will begin to

simmer. They will boil over. The WI will be urged to move even more quickly with the ribbon-making and some of them will complain of arthritis. The folk singer will break his wrist and will be unable to play his flageolet. The brass band will disband, making it an ex-brass band. The face painter will be sent to prison for using the wrong kind of paint at a Veteran's Luncheon. The minor celebrity will suddenly remember his prior booking and will try and wriggle out of the ribbon-snipping but will be presented with the contract he signed.

The village will be in turmoil and chaos. The ribbons will be thrown away. The oldest person in the village will be interrupted mid-anecdote and told to shut up. The whole festival will be abandoned in acrimony and hissing accusation. The Maypole will return to its rusty and unloved state. Until the next time somebody has a bright idea, of course. Take heed, readers, take heed.

Ah, the cricket season is in full flow; the summer game is at its zenith before the nights really start to draw in and autumn knocks at the door in a scarf and an outdoor coat. Village cricket grounds all over Yorkshire are resounding to the sound of willow on leather as the ball flies high into the sky like a spare moon, hanging for a moment before it falls into the grateful fielder's hands. How is he? He's out!

But, of course, the sound of willow on leather is only one of the noises we associate with cricket in Yorkshire. If we listen carefully we can hear many, many sounds vibrating across the county before the bat thwacks the ball. To start with, there's the sound of alarm clock on ear, as the captain of the third team is dragged out of bed by its insistent ringing after a long night in the cricket club bar; it was an evening of tactical discussion and weepy reminiscing about Geoff Boycott's hundredth hundred. Maybe too much beer was supped. Maybe the Chinese takeaway afterwards was an error. The cheesecake after the takeaway was most definitely an error.

Then there's the sound of hand on alarm clock, then there's the sound of ticking in the otherwise silent room. Ah, the cricket season is in full flow. Here's the sound of bacon landing in pan, of hot water glugging into teapot. Listen to the bacon sizzling in the kitchen air. Ah, the slurp of lips against cup, the subsequent drips and dribbles of tea against freshly-laundered cricket whites. The ringing of curses across the entire house as the drips of tea are

mopped up with a tea-towel, a novelty tea-towel of the sort that explains cricket to Americans.

The sound of bat falling into cricket bag. The sound of shoe on street as the captain walks down to the club. The sound of the captain's mobile phone on sweet morning air. The sound of excuses landing on deaf ears from the bloke who can't make it, then decides that he can make it because his wife suddenly announces that she's going to her sister's in Beverley for the day. The sound of relief on team sheet.

The sound of club door handle turning on club door. The sound of fist bumps and high fives as the early arrivals greet each other and shake their heads at last night's excesses, especially the cheesecake. The sound of brief summer rain on the club roof. The sound of weather apps being checked on phones. The sound of people saying to each other and to themselves: 'It's nowt. It'll pass over.'

The sound of the cricket tea being prepared. The sound of knife on butter on bread. The sound of ham slapped on buttered bread. The sound of cheese sliced and then slapped on buttered bread. The sound of cake being cut, a sweet geometry. The soft sifting sound of teabags tumbling into a vast club teapot the size of a Zeppelin.

The sound of tyres on car park. The sound of greetings and mumbled mutterings as more of the team arrive. The sound of tyres on car park. The sound of greetings and mumbled mutterings as the opposition arrive. The sound of forced jollity and jovial attempts at humorous blackmail and threats as the umpires arrive. The sound of brief summer rain on the club roof, soon passing over.

The sound of pad on leg, of shirt on back, of box on

tender area, of glove on hand, of helmet on head. The sound of friends and supporters arriving, setting out chairs, opening flasks, ordering beer at the bar. The sound of banter on deaf ear: 'Does tha want any cheesecake?' The sound of team talk on ears. The sound of slap on back. The sound of fist bumping on fist. The sound of captains walking across the sacred turf. The sound of coin turning and turning in the air. The sound of quid on grass. The sound of hand on hand, shaking firmly. The sound of fielding side walking out, led by captain. The sound of bat nervously poking grass. The sound of umpire commencing the match. And now, at last, the sound of the summer in Yorkshire, the sound of willow on leather, the ball as high in the air as a mission to Mars. Enjoy the rest of the season. How is he?

June in Yorkshire: a month of long, long days and short nights that seem to pass in the blink of an eye as you're gazing at the sky. A month of T-shirts and shorts and sandals with socks. A month when the middle-aged Yorkshireman gets his white flat cap out and sports it proudly on his walk to the shops. A month when the middle-aged Yorkshirewoman discards her cardigan, making it a discardigan, and shows her arms, invisible through winter and spring, to the sun.

June in Yorkshire: a month of hope for a fantastic summer, better than last year or the year before. If summer is the year's main course then June is its *amuse bouche* or tasting bit as they call it round here; a month to cleanse your palette from the harsh spring rain and prepare yourself for

the sweltering and heavy nights of July and August. A month of day trips to the seaside and tea rooms and cricket matches that always seem to go on for far too long and not for long enough at one and the same time.

June in Yorkshire: a month for instant nostalgia, for those Junes of your childhood that were warmer and brighter and somehow more full of promise. Or were they? Maybe June will always be full of promise because that's the kind of month it is, the Gateway to summer, the Back Door of spring. A fragile promise that you have to grasp because before you know it the year will be turning like that globe you used to have in Mrs Hinchliffe's class, the classroom with the pictures of the months on the wall, with June's image shining in both its own light and the light streaming through the window.

I had a friend at school called June and she emigrated to Australia and I'm sure she went in June, I'm sure I recall there being a June-shaped absence in the classroom one morning. I'm sure Mrs Hinchliffe said something like 'June's left us, but June's still here' but I might be making that up, I might be indulging in that instant nostalgia I mentioned earlier.

June in Yorkshire: sleep with the window open and listen to the sounds of the city or the town or the country, magnified by light and intensified by the fact that it's the early hours of the morning and you can still read without a torch. But the longest day comes and goes and then, imperceptibly, the year begins to turn and the year starts to decay ever so slightly. The nights start to draw in, only by a minute or so at a time, but the end of the month is different to the start of the month in terms of the difference between the light and the dark. Or is it a trick of the light? Or is it a trick of the dark? Or is it a trick of the calendar? Don't let it turn, you tell yourself, don't let it turn.

But it will. So, if you're reading this at the beginning of this most glorious month, enjoy the next few weeks as much as you can; if you're reading it the end, well wasn't it a fantastic June this year?

June in Yorkshire: time to get a petition going. Forget that 'Thirty days hath September, April, June and November' ditty. Let's give June a couple of extra days, at least. Thirty days hath September, and April and November, all the rest have thirty-one, except February which has twenty-eight and June in Yorkshire which has at least forty-two.

Maths isn't my strong point but as far as I'm concerned June is the strong point of the year. Enjoy!

No chance of wearing my shorts any more. No way can I go out of the house without my vest on. No stroll can be taken unless I scarf-up and hat-don. No light in the house can be left off after four o'clock in the afternoon. People of Yorkshire, welcome, through gritted and shivering teeth, to the month that hates to say Yes, to the festival of negativity that is November. In the late summer or early autumn, when there's a particularly foggy and chilly evening or morning, we'll say 'By, it's just like November' and everybody that we say it to knows exactly what we mean, and they shiver when we say it to them.

I was trying to fathom why I had such a downer (as the kids say) on the month, and then I recalled that old November poem by Thomas Hood that we did at school, the one that begins 'No sun, no moon/No morn, no noon/No dawn, no dusk, no proper time of day' and ends 'No fruits, no flowers, no leaves, no birds/ November!' and perhaps it's that particular piece of writing that made the month feel so much like its shaking its head and telling us we can't enjoy ourselves.

We had to learn the poem in Mrs Hinchcliffe's class and my (possibly faulty) memory is that, each year as October tripped up in the dark and slipped into November, the whole school would recite the poem in assembly just before Mrs Hudson played us out of the hall with Hills of the North Rejoice.

And it's true that this is certainly a month where the nights draw in and the days turn cold and damp and the glow of Christmas feels several streets away rather than just around the corner, although I have to say that when

my grandson was born on a cold November day a decade ago, it snowed, and for a moment Barnsley was like a Christmas card. But does November have to be the month that says No? Couldn't we, in Yorkshire at least, make it the month that says, if not Yes, than at least Maybe, or Perhaps?

After all, round here the 4th November is Mischief Night, a time when people like to say 'Yes?' as they open the door after you've knocked on it and run away; on Bonfire Night we like to say yes when people offer us another slice of parkin and we'll always say yes as we gaze up at a November full moon and people ask us if it's a beautiful sight. That's not enough, though; we need to find reasons to celebrate this month, to brush away the negativity and scrub the positivity in, which I'm sure was another song we used to sing at junior school.

Well, one reason to rejoice is that November really is deep autumn; it's autumn at its strongest and heaviest. A few hardy and stubborn leaves are still hanging on to the trees; berries are flooding the hedges like swarms of punctuation; the nights come quickly and the stars seem to shine more brightly. If there are three steps to autumn, then November is at the top. Winter is hanging around in the foyer, but autumn has centre stage because of Uncompromising November.

It's as though December is the brother that became a dancer, that likes to perform and act and sing, and November is the brother that became an artist, specialising in dark and heavy paintings that make you feel cold just to look at them. November makes sculptures that look and feel like slabs of metal, and December makes light and airy mobiles that glitter with frost. I'm not succeeding here, am I? I'm not even convincing myself that November is a good thing. Even in Yorkshire, we'll just have to put up with November, huddle round the bonfire, gaze up at the fireworks, reach for another jacket potato and look forward to spring. No Hawaiian shirts. No floaty frocks/No sunglasses. No summer socks. November.

Christmas — how much!?

It was late on a December evening, and the snow was starting to fall. Joe the joiner was a bit worried because he'd had to go back to his home town in the far reaches of the Dales to sign a bit of paperwork and their lass, little Mary, was heavily pregnant and he'd forgotten to book anywhere to stay which was maybe a bit silly at this time of year. Paperwork was the bane of Joe's life and that was maybe why he'd forgotten to book the room and also forgotten to have his car checked, and maybe that was why it had broken down ten yards from the end of the drive. Joe had come up with what he thought was a great idea; old Bess the Donkey from the back field. They could ride up the dale on her.

At first, Mary was against the idea but in the end she had to agree because they'd missed the last bus and there were no trains and that paperwork really needed to be done. So, reluctantly, she heaved herself onto Bess's back and they made their laborious way up the dale as night switched out the lights and the snow fell. Bess wasn't the most comfortable of rides and Mary kept thinking that maybe the baby would be coming early. Joe was getting a bit nervous about the accommodation and as they went through the villages he noticed the No Vacancies signs up at the B&Bs and the hotels.

Joe wasn't overwhelmingly nervous though, because he

We bring you All Gold, Frank's got incense and Merv's bought you a calendar

knew they'd get a room at the Red Lion in town. Joe and Mary had stayed at the Red Lion many times when they were courting, and it always amazed them how far the old pub went back, corridor after corridor stretching into a kind of Yorkshire infinity, and how many rooms there seemed to be. The snow was falling harder now, and Bess was getting tired. Joe comforted Mary with the fact that the Red Lion was only just ahead: he could see the sign, well lit and swinging in the breeze. He strode up to the door and walked in.

And then he walked out again. It was full. Full to the top with a fishing trip from Lancashire. There was no room at the Red Lion. Joe didn't use those words to Mary, though; he told her that the landlord had 'fixed them up with a place round the back' which Mary thought might mean a little room but which Joe knew meant a cowshed.

And that's how come Joe and Mary's little lad was born in the straw in a shed at the back of a pub on the coldest night of the year. Soon everybody got to hear about it and they all crowded round to take a look. Some shepherd lads off the high hills came down and just sat and stared, and there were tears in their eyes. And the pub quiz team from the Red Lion, known locally as the Three Clever Blokes, popped in on their way from thrashing the Dog and Duck and they gave the prizes they'd won to Mary and Jo and the babby. They weren't much, but the thought was there, and a baby can always make use of a box of after dinner mints, and a bottle of supermarket fizz, and a calendar of Hull by Moonlight. Even the Lancashire fishermen came and laid their tench on the floor in a lovely pattern. And because this is a sentimental Yorkshire Christmas story, they all sang sentimental Yorkshire Christmas songs until the next day.

My lovely wife and I have been married for thirty years. That's a Pearl Anniversary in most people's books, but of course a Firelighter Anniversary in Yorkshire. I got her some good ones from the market that really do get the flames going quickly with the minimum of spitting, and isn't that what you always want from a wedding anniversary, plenty of flames but not much spitting?

So I did okay with the anniversary, but then the question of Christmas looms like a cloud that threatens your picnic. I love Christmas but when you've known somebody for a

good slice of your life, what on earth do you get them? She's no help either. I asked her what she wanted for Christmas the other day when she was lighting the fire. 'A surprise,' she said, placing the coal carefully around the anniversary gift.

A surprise: that's no good, as I explained earlier in this book. I suppose I could dress up as Father Christmas with nothing on under the cloak and then leap out from behind the tree on Christmas morning shouting 'Boo!'. And holding the cloak wide. That would be a surprise. Especially if her mother had come round for a mince pie. Then, as I walked into an overdecorated shop and heard Christmas music being played incessantly, I had a great idea. Well, at the time I thought it was a great idea. Now, I'm not quite so sure.

I've got the pear tree: we've got one in the back garden, actually, so all I'll have to do is put a bit of tinsel on it. I've got a mate of mine to deliver a partridge to stick on top, like a feathery Christmas fairy. He promises it'll be there on Christmas Eve in good time. The turtle doves are easy too: they're the ones I hear cooing at the crack of dawn every day as I go for my stroll. They may not be turtle doves, actually. They might just be doves. I got a bit clever with the French hens: I'm going to make some chicken-and-garlic sandwiches. Three of 'em, of course. That's genius. The calling birds were slightly more difficult, especially as some sources say it's colly birds, but then I nipped next door and had a word with Mr Lowe and now, at a given signal, he'll stand in the garden and whistle four different tunes like four calling birds. He likes whistling, so that's okay.

I can't afford five gold rings, and anyway I'm a Yorkshireman so I've got one fake gold ring and four cardboard ones. I've made some geese-a-laying glove puppets and I've been secretly training our grandson Thomas to perform a Geese-a-Laying Dance. He says it makes his fingers hurt and that I've made the geese too big and heavy but I tell him it's Christmas and as the old Darfield saying goes, 'you can never have a goose too big for your fingers'.

I've got seven toy swans and they swim elegantly across our biggest pan. The humans are proving almost impossible to get hold of, though. To be frank, there aren't that many milkmaids in my part of the county and any lords that might be leaping must have leaped away because I don't come across many at the bus stop. So I've employed the local Amateur Dramatic Society, all of them, to make a living diorama. I had to pay them a bit to get them to turn up on Christmas Day but I promised I'd help to sponsor their next production of White Horse Inn. In return they're frantically making drummer or lady or piper or lord or maid costumes.

She wanted a surprise. She'll get a surprise.

I first saw a Christmas Shop in America a few years ago; they're a fairly regular feature of the landscape these days but at the time, in a small town in New England, they were a novelty and as we bought a Lyndon B Johnson bauble set I resolved to try and invent some Yorkshire Christmas items that would make me millions of Yorkshire pounds, which are like real pounds but grittier.

I filed the idea at the back of my mind together with my other Yorkshire-based money-making ideas (you know the ones I mean: Ilkley Moor Baht 'At re-recorded with a backbeat to make an unlikely Ibiza hit, and parkin-dispensing machines on every high street accessed via the Parkin Card, amongst others) until recently, when I revived the scheme because I'd hit on a brace of yuletide winners.

How's this for a start: the Yorkshire Snowman Template? How many boring snowmen do you see looking either like, well, blobs of snow, or chilly representations of the man you see on the fire exit sign or the gents' toilet door? Let's face it, what they lack is character, and that's where the Yorkshire Snowman Template comes in. Basically, it's a kind of hinged mould into which you can put snow, and which when opened will become a Snow Tyke. The mould includes a flat cap feature, a carefully designed muffler, and a detachable whippet which can be kept in a handy carrying case. Once the snow has been packed in as tightly as possible, the hinged mould is opened and as if by magic a Yorkshire Snowman is standing before you. During trials last winter, the White Rose Snowman Prototyke proved to be so realistic when I left it on the street that several people said 'Now then' to it, and one man from Tong shouted 'Where's that fiver you owe me?' at it, before taking a wild swing in the direction of the head, knocking it off, and having to be taken to the District General suffering

from Shaky Shock as my Auntie Mabel used to call it. Being a restless spirit I decided to expand my portfolio, as marketing people say. As a lad I always liked those snow globes, the ones that you turn over to make a blizzard in the comfort of your own home. I used to have one from New York with a little model of an NYPD cop car in it, and I sat and sketched out an idea for one that could be set in God's Own Country.

And now I can reveal my Christmas cracker of an idea. Look, here it is: Yes, I knew you'd be amazed. At first sight it just looks like an empty snow globe with no snow. A globe, in fact. In the background you can see a terraced house. Press this button on the side and the door opens in the house. Amazing, I know. A man in traditional Yorkshire shirt-sleeves emerges. He's not dressed for the cold but that's because he doesn't realise how cold it is. By an ingenious use of clockwork and minute tracks he makes his way to the centre of the globe. I know, I know; you're amazed at the workmanship.

Now press this button. Yes, that's right: audio! Listen: a woman's voice from inside the house ... 'George! Have you got your cap?' The capless one looks up at the slate-grey sky which I've suggested by the use of slate-grey paint. George shouts, 'Nay! I'll not need it!' and at that moment a hooter hoots and that's your cue to upend the globe and dump the solid mass of snow on the unfortunate George's head. It's a sure-fire Christmas winner and this time next year I'll be doing all my writing from Malibu.

When it comes to Christmas decorations, I'm old fash-ioned. I belong to the 'less is more' school of baubles and tinsel. I'm not a fan of the way that Yorkshire, during December, just becomes one big light that can be seen from the planet Neptune.

You know the kind of thing I mean: the house in the for-mer pit village transformed into a representation of the stable that the Christmas story began in, or in fact a repre-sentation of the stable that Disney might have created, or in fact a representation of the stable that Disney might have created while under the influence of Uncle Cecil's mulled wine. Then there's the phenomenon that psychia-trists (and we know where their minds wander to) call 'My tree's bigger than thine'. Trees that reach higher than cathedrals or Emley Moor mast, pointing up to heaven and tickling the angels. Fairies as big as the giant in Jack and the Beanstalk. Stars that are almost as huge as real stars that cause aircraft to be diverted from Leeds/Bradford airport.

Then there's the 'Santa Stop Here' sign, which is fine as a sign but not, I put it to you, as the kind of billboard you see by the side of the road in American cop shows. As far as I know Santa's eyes are fine; after all he sneaks some of Rudolph's carrots every now and then, so he doesn't need a sign that's bigger than an IMAX cinema screen or a Mount Rushmore head.

What's wrong with minimalism, anyway? There's less mess, I know that, as my mother would say. So, here's my Christmas proposal for a new type of decoration that will, in years to come, become the decoration of choice for the

Tha always has t go one better

discerning Tyke. It's exciting: keep this book because future historians will use it to reference where the New Decoration Revolution began. Here goes:

A bit of tinsel round your cap. Er …that's it. Simple genius: a bit of tinsel round your cap. Let me expand the idea, but only a little bit, because it's meant to be minimalist. Lots of Yorkshire chaps of a certain age still sport the flat cap in all weathers; it's a cultural symbol as much as a pate-warmer, it seems to me. It's saying: I'm Yorkshire, me. I'm Yorkshire through and through, tha knows. (This is despite the fact that people from lots of other counties and countries wear the flat cap. Somehow it symbolises

Yorkshire more than the Isle of Wight.) A bit of tinsel round your cap: perfect. So, all you have to do is get a length of tinsel, about six to nine inches will do, and fasten it around the top of your flat cap, from back to neb. Tie it on or Sellotape it on. If you're going to staple it on or hammer it on make sure you take the cap off first. Have a look at yourself in the mirror: perfect. Christmassy but not too Christmassy. Stylish but not showy.

Perhaps the first time you walk out with it on you'll feel a bit silly, but that feeling will soon pass like the mist over Crackpot. You'll soon see other flat-cappers wearing the Tinsel Top, as it will become known. Ladies: don't feel left out: tinsel round the headscarf is an acceptable alternative. Posh people who aren't from Yorkshire: tinsel round the bowler hat will do. People who don't wear a hat of any kind and who aren't from Yorkshire: just tie a bit of tinsel round your head and then we can laugh at you next time you come to God's Own Country.

Remember: not too much, lights not needed, result superb. Now, where did I put that tinsel and that stapler?

Ah, we all remember that bad winter, don't we? You know the one, that really bad winter. That winter when it was, frankly, really bad. I'm hedging my bets because whenever you talk to anybody from Yorkshire they'll always have their own version of The Worst Winter. 1963? Balmy and sub-tropical, you should have been here in 1948. 1948? That was a heatwave compared to 1921 … and so it goes on. If pressed, though, a lot of Yorkshire folk will agree that the worst winter ever round these parts was 1887; nobody alive remembers it, of course, but it's passed into folk memory and legend as The Winter the Words Frozz for Christmas.

It wasn't as though December 1887 had been particularly bad until the latter end of the month and then, overnight on 20th-21st December, a gale blew in from Siberia and covered the whole of the county with a flat cap of snow. I'm saying 'flat cap of snow', by the way, because I see it as the writer's task to renew the language and aren't we all fed up of reading the phrase 'blanket of snow'? Yes we are.

Anyway, the wind blew over from the east and Yorkshire woke up to a muffler of snow. Rumours that a Siberian peasant was blown all the way to Pickering persisted for years in that area, but have now been dismissed

as hearsay, even though a number of citizens of that fine town are adept at the Cossack dance. As Christmas approached conditions became worse; roads, which were not all that passable at the best of times, became completely impassable. Railways ground to a halt. Factories, mills and mines were shut because the workers couldn't get there to be exploited. People huddled in their homes trying to find new ways of describing the white scenes outside their windows; a blanket of snow? Heard it before. A flat cap of snow? Too daft. A muffler of snow? Getting closer.

And then, because it got so cold, a weather-related phenomenon occurred that was almost without precedent since the ice age; scientists call it a linguistic extreme temperature incident, but of course we refer to it as the aforementioned, The Winter the Words Frozz for Christmas.

People noticed that as they spoke, nobody could hear what they said and, in fact, they couldn't actually get the words out. They'd open their mouths to say 'By, it's really cold tha knows' and the words would instantly form a kind of lollipop-cum-iceberg which would tumble from their lips and sit on the floor like a tiny snowman. An opera singer in Halifax tried to sing a long note and found that his entire room was transformed into an icy wonderland. A hardy priest ventured to his little church high on the moors, delivered his sermon to the empty pews and was found the next day perched on a white mountain of quotes, texts, lessons and imprecations.

People attempted to sing Christmas carols to keep themselves warm and the result was a kind of snowball fight, with frozen versions of Good King Wenceslas flying around shivery front parlours like cold white moths. The cold spell lasted until well into the New Year, when luckily a warm front thawed out the snow-bound county. And the words unfroze, causing hilarity and not a few arguments. Did he really say that to her? Was that meant to be public knowledge? Was that singing really so dreadfully out of key?

But the really mysterious thing is that, by chance, some words remain frozen. Perhaps they'd ended up down the bottom of a really cold cellar in a big house or one of those ice-houses that they had in country mansions. A couple of amateur scientists kept whole paragraphs frozen in primitive fridges, and one man from Hull took an entire conversation with him when he emigrated to Switzerland.

And now, at Christmas, when we're covered with a sheet of snow, maybe it's time to remember The Winter the Words Frozz for Christmas, and perhaps thaw out a couple of the remaining sentences just to see what we used to sound like.

Merry Christmas to everyone. Say those words aloud in a chest freezer, freeze them, and keep them till next year.

On the first day of Yorkshire Christmas my true love gave to me A Racing Pigeon in a privet hedge.

On the second day of Yorkshire Christmas my true love gave to me Two Whippy Whippets and A Racing Pigeon in a privet hedge.

On the third day of Yorkshire Christmas my true love gave to me Three Yorkshire Terriers, Two Whippy

Whippets and A Racing Pigeon in a privet hedge.

On the fourth day of Yorkshire Christmas my true love gave to me Four Slices of Parkin and the other stuff I've sung about before.

On the fifth day of Yorkshire Christmas my true love gave to me Five Golden Yorkshire Puds and the rest of the gifts that now are piling up in my parlour next to the leather-effect settee and threatening Uncle Stan's view of the telly.

On the sixth day of Yorkshire Christmas my true love gave to me Six Flat Cap Wearers called Jim and the items that I've already described.

On the seventh day of Yorkshire Christmas my true love gave to me Seven Lovely Curd Tarts and the rest of the boxes and parcels, some of them squawking, that are now taking up an inordinate amount of space in all the rooms of my house to such an extent that I've not caught a glimpse of Uncle Stan for at least eighteen hours, although I can sometimes hear his feeble cries and knockings.

On the eighth day of Yorkshire Christmas my true love gave to me Eight Mufflered Old Blokes backing up to the house in a minibus and almost crushing some of the other presents that are scattered on the drive because there's no room for them anywhere else seeing as I only live in a small terraced house.

On the ninth day of Christmas my true love gave to me Nine Life Size Dickie Bird Statues as well as all the other things I've already listed and it took a huge removal van to bring them I can tell you and I tried to make the driver a cup of tea but I think the Whippy Whippets may have smashed it; they're certainly making their presence felt in other ways, too, if you get my drift. Uncle Stan seems to have completely disappeared; I thought I saw him a day or two ago but it was just the shadow of the racing pigeon in the privet hedge.

On the tenth day of Yorkshire Christmas my true love gave to me ten boxes of Ee By Gum, the special adhesive that, as the advertising slogan goes, 'makes everything stick like a Yorkshireman sticks to his wallet' as well as all the other rammel mentioned in the previous lines of this ditty. You don't need me to tell you that the PR company that came up with that slogan came from Lancashire.

On the eleventh day of Yorkshire Christmas my true love gave to me Eleven Tons of Fresh White Roses and all the rest of the list of gifts already presented to this hapless recipient and I have to say that for a moment I thought it was snowing as all the rose petals drifted around the street.

On the twelfth day of Yorkshire Christmas my true love gave to me twelve Brass Bands Playing Ilkley Moor Bah't 'At, Eleven Tons of Fresh White Roses, Ten Boxes of Ee By Gum, Nine Life Size Dickie Bird Statues, Eight Mufflered Old Blokes, Seven Lovely Curd Tarts, Six Flat Cap Wearers called Jim, Five Golden Yorkshire Puds, Four Slices of Parkin, Three Yorkshire Terriers, Two Whippy Whippets and a Racing Pigeon in a Privet Hedge.

There's a car boot sale in the next village on Boxing Day: I'll see you there. I'll get Uncle Stan to drive. If I can locate him.

I always think the best thing about Christmas in Yorkshire is that there's a kind of temporal routine. In other words things happen at the same time; you can set your clock by them, unless your clock's broken and you're hoping for a new one for Christmas.

So, we know that Christmas is coming when the shops start selling baubles and decorations in early September, we know that Christmas is coming when, in mid-October, the kids write their War and Peace-sized lists, and we know that Christmas is coming when, in early December, the dog eats all the chocolates from the advent calendar. These are general pre-Christmas events, of course, but each reader will have a time-period that's special to them and their loved ones.

It might involve carol singing round the tree, or fighting

over a turkey leg, or pretending to be enthusiastic about comedy socks. You do them at the same time every year and without them, well, Christmas isn't really Christmas, is it?

In our family, one of the great Christmas time-zones occurred on Boxing Day, which some would argue wasn't really part of Christmas at all, but I think it is. Each Boxing Day something happened at Uncle Jack's house in Sheffield that informed us it was time to get our coats on and drive home slowly through the swirling Yorkshire sleet. We always went to Uncle Jack and Auntie Mary's place on Boxing Day and we enjoyed a sumptuous tea and pulled crackers and maybe got a late present or two.

Then we'd see Uncle Jack wink at Auntie Mary and he'd disappear into their small kitchen. Did I catch the slight breath of a long-suffering sigh from Auntie Mary? Surely not, not at a time of goodwill to all men, especially those called Jack. Or maybe I did. Just a slight breath.

Uncle Jack would reappear, his cracker-hat slightly askew, with a plate of biscuits, small buns and mince pies. 'Shall we have summat sweet to finish us off?' he'd say, in a jolly tone. He'd proffer the plate to my dad, who knew what he had to do, because what was happening with the plate was part of a long tradition that went back years. My dad's hand would hover over the biscuits and buns but then he'd say, 'Do you know, I think I'll have a jam mince pie.' My mother would do the same: the hovering, the eventual choosing of the mince pie. My brother, a rebellious teenager, almost chose a two-fingered Kit-Kat but a dagger-stare from my mother guided his hand towards the mince pies. The plate came to me. The mince pies gleamed in the firelight. They looked so …inviting. I picked one up.

At this point Uncle Jack would barely be able to conceal his volcanic mirth. He'd put his big hands over his mouth to stop the laughter rushing into the room and spoiling the annual joke. You see, the joke was that they weren't real mince pies. They were rubber mince pies bought from a back street joke shop. Jack had tried them out on the McMillans before I was born and they'd been such a hit that he'd done it every year since. It was the tea-party equivalent of The Great Escape, and me taking a chomp out of a rubber mince pie once again was like Steve McQueen failing to get over the barbed wire on that bike once again.

I bite into the pie. It tastes like a new shoe from a

discount shoe shop. 'Hey, Uncle Jack, this pie's a bit rubbery!' I say. 'So is mine!' my mother says, laughing. 'Mine too!' my dad splutters. My brother says nothing and pretends to eat his. 'I'll tell you why,' Uncle Jack shouts, triumphantly. 'It's because they're not real mince pies, not real mince pies at all! I'll tell you what: they're rubber! Flipping rubber!' just like he does every year.

We laugh and get our coats. The Christmas rubber-tart clock has chimed. Time to go back home. Merry Christmas, everybody; may all your mince pies be real ones.

Wait for a good, generous snowstorm; one of those where the snow tumbles from the sky like Lux flakes. Wait for a good, generous snowstorm that lasts for hours, until the roads are covered and the street becomes a snow-street, glowing orange in the streetlights like a lollipop. Once the snow has stopped, or even as it's still falling, get your wellies on and your big coat and your woolly hat and run out into the garden. Your feet sink into the fresh snow to a depth you wouldn't have thought possible. Or maybe it's just that you're short.

Make a snowball. Roll it and roll it until it gets huge. Ah, this is exciting. This is really exciting; thank you, snow, for dropping onto my garden! This is the perfect amount of precipitation to make a Snow Yorkshireman! We know all about the making of snowmen, about the fat melting blokes in the garden with their carrot noses and their buttons of coal; anybody can make a snowman, but the making of Snow Yorkshiremen is a much more refined and skilful art, that some say is dying out but which I know is undergoing something of a revival. Well put it this way, the last time we had snow I saw quite a few of them proudly and magnificently dotting the gardens and fields of Yorkshire.

Making a Snow Yorkshireman is much more than making a snowman, of course. The tricky bits of a Snow Yorkshireman are the flat cap, the muffler, and the arms outstretched as though the figure is saying How Much?, in the traditional Tyke style. The maker of these chilly objects is more of a sculptor than anything else, and the difference between a Snow Yorkshireman and the traditional Snowman is like the difference between a cave painting and the Sistine Chapel.

As a skilled Yorkshire Snowman artisan builder, I have to admit that I feel nothing but contempt for the hobbyists who spend their winters making ordinary snowmen,

165

simply because they don't apply themselves with enough rigour to the craft that is really an art. The prime example of this is the carrot nose; for me that's just an example of sloppy thinking and laziness. If you want a nose, make one from snow. It's obvious really. If you want your snowman to have a hat, don't get one from the dressing-up box or from the pegs at the bottom of the stairs: mould one, create your own, like I have to do with the flat cap.

Get your ball of snow, the one that will make the body, and place the smaller ball of snow, the head-ball as it's technically known, on top. So far so simple. Now comes the difficult bit, the bit that you have practised for years. Get enough snow in your cupped hands to make a flat cap and begin the shaping process: the neb, the round bit at the back, the essential and yet somehow poetic flatness. Press the snow together; if you were writing a poem about a flat cap you would make many drafts and it's the same when you're moulding a snow flat cap for your Snow Yorkshireman. Some attempts will crumble.

Some will look nothing like a flat cap. Persist. You have trained for this moment. That's the flat cap done. Place it on the head of the Snow Yorkshireman. The snow muffler is more difficult, but be patient. Do not let your concentration waver, as the old masters say, and your muffler will be perfect. And it is.

But now comes the really hard part, the making of the snow arms outstretched as if to say How Much!?. Some people, I've heard, will insert pieces of wood or metal into their Snow Yorkshireman's shoulders to make a kind of framework around which they can mould the snow to make the How Much!? arms. This is pathetic. After what is admittedly a long apprenticeship in extreme snowman-making, taking decades from your life, you should be able to make freestanding arms that will survive from Christmas to at least until the thaw sets in.

Anyway, I can't stand here blathering on: I've got a Snow Yorkshireman to make before the snow gets too hard. I'll sing as I mould. All together now: 'Tha flying through t' air, tha knows … .'

When Ah worra lad

My mother used to tell me off for doing nothing in September. I'd be sitting on the settee towards the end of the long summer holidays and I'd be reading Biggles of 266 Squadron for the fifteenth time; well, half-reading it. My eyes would land on a word and they'd kind of graze on it like an uncle at a wedding buffet in Cleckheaton; after a while I'd try to move to another word, perhaps to take in a sentence or two, but the effort would be just too much. If I'd understood what the word languorous meant then that's how I would have said I was feeling. Languorous, tha knows. She'd have to send me round to Mrs Batty's for a cut loaf to stop me getting settee-sores.

I guess it was partly the late summer heat of the late 1960s that induced this feeling of torpor; that, and the fact that the new school term was approaching like the 37 bus when it loomed out of the mist: you knew it was coming because you could hear it and you could discern a kind of bus-shaped smudge in the distance, but you never quite believed it until it was suddenly next to the bus stop and Alvin the driver was gesturing at you to get on.

It was like that with the new term: a long way away in the mist then suddenly there, suddenly waiting, suddenly gesturing at you because you were late. My theory was that if I sat and did nothing for the last couple of weeks of the holidays, then it would never come. I was wrong. Despite this, I love September in Yorkshire, and I love the way it arrives with more of a nudge than a slap in the chops.

I stand in the garden every morning clutching my mug of Assam tea with the teabag still in and I gaze at the trees at the bottom of the garden. I can hear the cars going along Doncaster Road and I can discern a distant aircraft making its way to Leeds Bradford Airport; I can hear a gate opening and closing up the street and I can hear the paper boy's

can you ring back, Ian's checking for signs of Autumn

bicycle going by and if I stand really still I can hear the distant chicka-chicka of his iPod disappearing up the street. Then it strikes me that yesterday morning I couldn't hear the same things quite so clearly, and I know that autumn is here. That's how it is for me: a sudden clarity of sound, the heaviness of the August air suddenly thinning to the hint of a chill. I'll glug my tea and take a deep breath and I can feel autumn in my lungs; a slight promise of bonfires and turnip lanterns and streetlights and frost. Of course, those things are still weeks and months away but they're waiting in the wings. They're on their way. I stand for a moment longer in the garden, then I go back into the house and put the kettle on again.

And the rest of the year will happen like a big machine clicking into action: the autumn football matches with moments of heroism and farce under floodlights; the nights that get darker earlier, and the sudden clear evenings where you can see your breath and it obscures the stars; the paper boy's iPod murmuring in the morning half-dark, and the way my grandson starts to talk about Christmas.

For now, though, I'll take another cup of tea into the garden and savour the first moments of autumn. I'll look at the huge tree at the back of our garden, the one I mark the seasons with, and see if any leaves really are starting to turn. If I stand long enough I might be able to capture the moment when the green weakens and the brown starts to assert itself. That'll take a few more cups of tea, of course. Languorous, tha knows.

When I was a lad growing up in Darfield, this time of year meant two things: scarves and Bonfire Night. My mother had a theory that October was really still the back end of summer, but once we turned the calendar to November then we were in the middle of winter and it was time to get the scarves out. I really didn't like scarves, partly because they were so easy to lose. My mother would make sure I had it on in the morning, by winding it round my neck so tightly that my head turned blue and my eyes bulged and I walked down to Low Valley Juniors looking like a strange species of fish, but many's the time I left it in the boys' cloakroom or unwound it on the Inkerman fields on the way home to use as a lasso in a game of Lone Ranger and never saw it again. So she knitted me another or bought one from Mr Walker the credit tailor who knocked on the door every Friday at about twelve o'clock.

Bonfire Night was, let's face it, more exciting than scarves. It had been on our personal horizon since the end of the summer holidays, to be honest, when we'd discussed the fireworks we'd buy and the size of our bonfires. In those days, the early 1960s, the communal organised bonfire was unheard of. Every back garden would have its own blaze and its own little display of fireworks, shooting and fizzing in the air briefly as pitmen on the early shift turned uncomfortably in bed and then decided to get up and join the fun. We'd eat roast potatoes and parkin and bonfire toffee and we'd burn a guy and I have vivid memories of my dad's face lit up by the flames as he stood well back and lit the blue touch paper on a Vesuvius.

As mentioned before, Uncle Charlie worked down Houghton Main pit and he wasn't a big fan of Bonfire Night. He thought it was too noisy and I reckon that subconsciously he was disappointed that we were burning wood, not coal. He really hated jumping crackers, in particular. I'm not sure why. He once referred darkly to the Sheffield blitz but that was odd because he'd never been to

Oh how the family laughed when young Ian mistook Uncle Charlie for a scarf

Sheffield. We had to warn him when we were setting one off and he'd go and sit in the back room till it had stopped jumping. Except one year.

It must have been one of my brother's mates, with a gleam in his eye, who put the jumping cracker under the kitchen chair that Uncle Charlie insisted on sitting on in the garden to watch the fireworks. My brother's mate leaned over and lit the jumping cracker with a match and then walked nonchalantly away, whistling the theme from Davy Crockett. I'd never seen Uncle Charlie move so fast as the cracker began to fizzle and bang. He looked, for a moment, like he was dancing a strange kind of ritual dance. His braces came loose and they flapped around him and he lifted his long legs high in the air like a ballet dancer. His glasses flew off and turned and turned in the night sky. And I clearly remember thinking, as Uncle Charlie bent and twisted and tried to escape, that he looked like a scarf moving in the breeze. 'He looks like a scarf,' I said to nobody in particular. Perhaps that was the moment I became a poet, when I hit on simile, when I realised that something could look like something else. Thanks, Uncle Charlie.

Now, don't tell anybody, but I once did a very bad thing. A very bad thing to do with language. I invented a Yorkshire word and didn't tell anybody that I'd made it up. Well, not for a while, anyway. And then when I did confess it just made things worse.

Let me explain: when I was about thirteen, four long decades and a bit ago, I became obsessed with Yorkshire words. I liked to roll words like brussen and sithi around my tongue. I liked the way they felt in my mouth, like hard Yorkshire Mixtures or crisp Yorkshire puddings. I speculated about the origin of dialect words, about how they might have been suddenly coined by a farmer in a moment of stress on a rainy moor, or thoughtfully spoken by someone trying to describe the exact way that light falls on a barn roof. I was young and daft, and I decided to make my mark on Yorkshire language, figuring that it would give me a kind of immortality, that it could be like a statue or a portrait or a blue plaque. How wrong I was.

I wrote to the local paper under a pseudonym, pretending that my old Yorkshire granddad often used the word 'booley' to describe something he didn't like very much, as in 'That's a booley wind that's blowing round the backs' or 'I feel a bit booley this morning: I think I'm catching a cold'. The paper published the letter and then I got some of my mates to write in using false names and claiming different derivations and exact meanings for the word.

The next week they all appeared in the letters page along with a couple of real answers. I was amazed. Somehow the word that I'd thought up as I was eating some chips and beans one autumn teatime had become a real thing, alive and slippery like an eel. I wrote another letter, bolder now, suggesting that my granddad had first heard the word from his dad who came from North Yorkshire and who moved to South Yorkshire to work down the pit. The letter was published and the week after more replies trickled in; one from me writing as Seth Gomersall and a couple from real people.

I was simultaneously excited and horrified. I felt that I was refreshing the dialect but that I was also committing some unspecified crime against language; I felt proud that somewhere on a Yorkshire street someone was saying 'By, I feel a bit booley this morning, tha knows', but I also felt nervous that some professor of Yorkshireness somewhere or other was ransacking his filing cabinet of words and finding that booley was nowhere to be seen.

So, almost weeping, I wrote to the paper and explained what I'd done. I pleaded youth and sacklessness. I promised I wouldn't do it again. I said that I knew I was a bad lad and, in a foolish afterthought said that I felt quite booley about the whole thing, which rather negated the

'Ian ... er the Booley family are here, they want a word'

contrite tone of the rest of the letter. The editor wrote an annoyed letter back, telling me (in quite officious language that made me think that somehow I'd end up doing a stretch in the Grammar Wing at Armley) that I was daft and irresponsible and that I shouldn't deceive people about important things like words.

And that was that. Or so I thought. But the other day I was on a train somewhere in Yorkshire (let's call it Xthorpe, not to be confused with Hexthorpe, which is part of Doncaster) and I heard somebody say 'That sky looks a bit booley, don't you think?'. My chest swelled with pride and my heart pounded. I felt like an astronomer who finds out that star he discovered hasn't gone out after all. My word, hanging in the air like dust in the sun. My word, still alive after all these years. I wonder how it got there: I wonder how it journeyed from that local paper letters page in the late 1960s to that man's vocabulary in the twenty-first century? I guess I'll never know, and I didn't ask. But I'll tell you how it makes me feel: booley marvellous!

In the late 1960s August was the time of year when Uncle Charlie always decided he should get his car out and go on his holidays. This seems like a fairly normal thing to do, but of course it wasn't for Uncle Charlie. Most of the year he was happy with his routine: go to work at the pit. Come home from the pit. Sit on the settee. Tell me that Clem Attlee was the best prime minister we ever had. Have his tea. Go to bed. Get up. Go to the pit.

In August, something always clicked in Uncle Charlie's soul. It could have been the sun on his back as he walked home from Houghton Main after a day shift. It could have been the way the heat made his head prickle under his heavy flat cap. It could have been the postcard his son, Little Charlie, an early adopter of package holidays, sent from Spain, or it could have just been the fact that, even for Uncle Charlie, a routine would eventually pall.

So he would go and open his garage and get his car out. His old Ford Anglia, as green as the blazers of a minor public school, with the registration number 4095 HE. He'd tell me, as I sat watching Ten Town on his big black and white telly, to go and tell my dad that him and Auntie (she was really Auntie Gladys but we always just called her Auntie) were going to come with us on our holidays, and my heart would sink. Uncle Charlie would probably have been banned from the roads these days, or he'd have been the subject of a reality TV show called Yorkshire's Worst Drivers. He was as good a driver as I am. And I can't drive.

I went to tell my dad, who, unlike Uncle Charlie, was a meticulous preparer of holidays. He'd look in a brochure for a nice guest house in Bridlington. He'd book a room for him and my mam and my brother and me. He'd send off a postal order. He'd send for a route map from the AA. He'd have the car checked. He'd buy a new shirt and a new tie for his holidays. Uncle Charlie would just turn up and end up staying in a room above a barber's in the Latin Quarter or in a caravan that had probably seen service in the Peninsular War. That's the First Peninsular War.

When my dad got the news that Uncle Charlie and Auntie were coming with us he'd look up, momentarily, at the ceiling, and then his natural optimism would take over. 'Oh well,' he'd say, 'he'll buy the fish and chips one night!' And that was that. We got ourselves a convoy, as the old country song said.

Uncle Charlie couldn't read or write, which never seemed to bother him very much and he resisted all my attempts to teach him. I even showed him some copies of *Dalesman* because he loved Yorkshire almost as much as he loved Clement Attlee. 'Lovely pictures, kid!' he'd say. 'Yes, but you can read about the places in the pictures,' I'd say. 'What's the point of reading about 'em when I can look at 'em?' he'd say, and that was that. Because he couldn't read, he always got lost. Road signs and street signs meant nothing to him. 'You can always ask somebody,' he'd say. That's true, but Uncle Charlie's Barnsley accent was so rich that baffled people in North Yorkshire villages must have often thought they were being spoken to by a man from Finland in a flat cap.

The other eccentric thing about Uncle Charlie was that he enjoyed driving backwards. 'It seems to be easier to steer,' he'd say to my horrified dad. It was true: if he was just nipping to the shop on the corner he'd seem to find it simple to whizz up North Street backwards, making it South Street, I guess.

On the morning of the holiday we'd call by Uncle Charlie's. Our car was piled up to the top with clothes and beach stuff and picnic stuff, and me and my brother were squashed in the back, our faces pressed up against the glass. Auntie and Uncle Charlie weren't quite ready. 'We'll be along later,' he'd say, airily.

And that is why the legend persists in certain villages throughout North Yorkshire: the legend of the day at the end of a decade when a car driven by a tall gesticulating man in a flat cap rattled backwards down the main street and disappeared in a cloud of dust. That was no legend. That was Uncle Charlie.

At this moment (if you're reading this on a Sunday night) happy parents all over Yorkshire are tucking the kids up between the sheets and uttering the time-honoured phrase that takes on an extra resonance at this time of year: 'School in the morning!' and the kids are groaning and turning over in bed and dreaming of days on the beach and nights staying up late. Bunting can be detected in some windows and one family who've got three lads of junior school age have hired a brass band and a male voice choir which seems just a little bit over the top, but then again, with three junior school lads, maybe not.

Yep, it's September and the long summer holiday is just about over. It feels like just a minute ago that it was July and the schools were breaking up and the kids were coming home with all their work from the last term in a folder and their eyes full of the promise of six weeks of freedom. And now the school bell is ringing, and it's going to be a long haul till October half term.

I started school in 1960, a time that feels so long ago that it ought to be in black-and-white and accompanied by a posh newsreel voiceover. In the weeks before the first day, my excitement rose and rose like steam in a kettle until I could hardly contain it. I asked my mother over and over again what school would be like and she tantalised me with meaningless phrases like 'Wait and see!' or 'You'll soon be the little scholar!' and my dad told me about how he used to walk four miles to school and four miles back and he once won a prize for writing an essay on the League of Nations. My mother, when she'd run out of wise phrases, told me about how she once walked to school in her best Sunday dress and fell in a sewerage works and had to run all the way home. All these well-meaning homilies and anecdotes just confused me even more until I thought that school was a place miles away that smelt of sewerage and was full of essays, whatever they were. In fact, because it was years before I saw the word 'essay' written down, I thought it was spelled S A and I had no idea what it stood for.

On the Sunday before my first day at Low Valley Infants I was whirling around in a state of what people from Muker call 'Reeth Giddiness' and people from Reeth call 'Muker Jumpiness'. My parents decided to take me and my brother to see Grandma in Great Houghton to calm me down. She wasn't my real grandma, of course: it was Yorkshire in the days before BBC2, after all.

She was renowned for her coconut cakes; for their consistency, which was like that of a breeze block, and their taste, which was like that of CS gas. We got to her house and she said to me and my brother, 'I know what you lads would like: some lovely coconut cake,' gesturing at a charred and smoking cinder on the table. We tried to escape, running out of the back door past my mother's despairing grasp and we scaled the wall at the back of Grandma's yard, running along bricks as solid as her cakes. I slipped. I slipped like an Olympic skater in a final and crashed to the ground and hit my head and knocked myself daft. Stars whirled round my head as though I was in the *Dandy*. And that's why I started school three days late. 'School in the morning' meant Wednesday for me. And that's why I've always been three days behind. It was the coconut cake that set me back.

When I was a lad I remember my dad showing me a photograph of an old-fashioned bike; it was a funny-looking contraption with no pedals and it was being ridden by somebody who looked like an extra from a Sunday teatime costume drama. 'That bike's called a MacMillan's Hobby Horse,' my dad said proudly, 'and even though we're McMillan not MacMillan, it's nice to have something named after you, even if it's a bike with no pedals and even if the name is slightly different.'

I got what he meant: to have something named after you, even at one remove and with a different spelling, ensures a kind of immortality. Ask Mr Hoover. Or Mr Biro. Or Mr Rolls. Or Mr Royce. Or Mr Hargreaves. Well,

maybe not Mr Hargreaves: his self-lighting fish-oil lamp never really caught on.

So, as I enter middle-age, my ambition is to leave my name somewhere for ever. And, because I'm a proud Yorkshireman, I want to have something in this great county named after me, so that years after my death I'll be remembered in some small way. The question is, what should I choose? There are so many possibilities out there. I can understand why philanthropists often want their names on the hospital wings or the football stadiums or the libraries that they've donated to: if you can't have your name up in lights, at least you can have it up in bricks.

So, what if I made a variation on that great Yorkshire

delicacy, the curd tart? How about if I added a sausage to the top, thus creating a dish that was both main course and pudding at the same time? And instead of calling the culinary delight Curd Tart with a Sausage on Top, we could call it McMillan's Curd Tart. Hungry people in shops would say, 'I'll have a curd tart, please: make it a McMillan's.'

Or what if I came up with a new way of walking across the North York Moors? How about if, instead of simply putting one foot in front of the other which is, I freely admit, the normal method of perambulation, you always lifted your knees as high in the air as you possibly could every time you took a step, as though you were pulling your feet away from chewing gum on an urban pavement, and at the same time waved your arms as in a tic-tac-man or 'Help, I'm drowning in syrup' kind of way? This way of traversing rough country in Yorkshire could be known as a McMillan. 'I'm just going for a stroll on the moors, dear.' 'How far will you be walking?' 'Oh, I'm not walking, I'm McMillaning.' Guaranteed immortality.

What could be more Yorkshire than a flat cap? But how about if I invented a flat cap with flaps? A flap cap, in other words. The flaps would be concealed under the neb of the cap until it started to drizzle and then the flaps would be liberated from the neb and, hey presto! Dry ears. I'd patent the item and, like the Duke of Wellington, the Earl of Cardigan, and George Vest of Beverley, I'd have my name forever attached to an item of clothing. 'By, it looks like rain so I'll not bother taking my cap, I'll put my McMillan on.'

Imagine somebody in North Yorkshire in the distant future going for a walk in the rain and then popping into a café for some sustenance. They would turn to their loved one and say, 'I'm going for a nice bracing McMillan on the tops. Have you seen my McMillan? It looks like rain. I won't be late back but I won't want any tea because I'm going to have a McMillan in the café. I might even have two. Do you want one bringing back?'

I'll be smiling down from somewhere, satisfied in the knowledge that my name lives on, if only in curd tarts, methods of walking and flat cap appendages. Well, even Thomas Crapper had to start somewhere.

Bonfire night was always a big culinary celebration in our house; for once, in the evening, we'd be allowed to forego the traditional meat-and-two-veg and go for something exciting and exotic. I'm talking hot dogs here, you realise. Well, this was Yorkshire in the 1960s. Hot dogs were only just off the ration, or so my parents would have me believe, and this added to their rarity value.

There was even a rumour one year that Uncle Jack would be bringing some mustard, although in the end he just brought Henderson's Relish which was exotic enough for us, I can tell you. I was glad he didn't bring any mustard because I confided to my brother that thousands of soldiers had been killed by mustard in the First World War. He confided in me that it was actually mustard gas. I fought back tears, more or less successfully.

There was also the fact that we didn't have to sit round the table on Bonfire Night and eat from plates with knives and forks; casual dining was okay in the middle of the day but in our house we had our evening meal all together, sitting, holding cutlery. On Bonfire night we could go outside in the dark. We could eat hot dogs sprinkled with Henderson's Relish. We could have more than one hot dog and we had a bit of tissue to wipe the grease from our chin.

It didn't stop at hot dogs, of course. One year we had burgers, too. One year we had pork pies that were so big you could have hollowed them out and lived in them. We always had parkin with that unique nutty taste that seems to get diluted a bit when you eat it at the same time as your hot dog. We didn't care: it was liberty hall. The Lord of Misrule was, well, misruling and he was a Yorkshireman called Guy Fawkes. Henderson's Relish on your parkin? Why not!

Then one year, a couple of days before 5th November, my mam announced an addition to the Bonfire menu: jacket potatoes. It's hard for me now, as a sophisticated man of the world who knows which end to hold his grapefruit spoon and how to order a cup of tea in three languages, to recall the fact that, in 1965, I had no idea what a jacket potato was. A potato was either a chip waiting to happen, or was incomplete until you mashed it with a fork. What the heck was a jacket potato?

I could have asked my brother of course, but I was still smarting from the mustard gaffe, so I kept quiet. I tried to think what it could possibly be. I'd seen somebody's dog wearing a tartan rug a couple of days before: maybe that was it. Maybe the potato was covered in some kind of protective coat, making it a jacket potato. Maybe it had

Well Ian, tha looks smart enough t' meet a King Edward

somehow been jacked-up in the oven, like a car got jacked-up in the garage. If the potato was higher in the oven maybe it would cook more quickly, or something.

Maybe it wasn't jacket potato: maybe it was Jackie potato. Perhaps the dish was named after somebody who looked like a potato, or somebody who had invented a new way of cooking the humble spud?

November the 5th arrived and as my dad went out to work he said, 'See you later! I'm looking forward to my jacket potato!' Suddenly I knew what it was: my dad always went to work in a jacket and tie and a jacket potato was one you had to wear a jacket to eat. It was a kind of formal informality, if you like. So that night when we were almost ready to go out and eat, I went upstairs and put the jacket on I wore for church every week. I looked very smart. I looked ready, in my jacket, for my jacket potato.

I'll leave it there, if that's okay. I won't mention the cruel laughter round the fire. I won't mention my brother saying 'Is that your mustard jacket?' I won't mention Uncle Jack saying 'Careful! Don't get any relish down those sleeves!'.

And I won't mention my mam bringing out a plate of potatoes with skins on.

It would have been many springs ago, sometime in the early 1960s in Low Valley Primary School. Mrs Hudson held up a photograph of an animal with long ears and asked us what it was. My hand went up with loads of other hands and Mrs Hudson picked me. I swelled with pride and said, 'A rabbit, Mrs Hudson. And we've got one at home and it's called Bunny Fluff.' When the laughter died down Mrs Hudson said, 'That's close, Ian, but not quite right,' and Sheryl Lang said it was a hare and Mrs Hudson gave her a star. Mrs Hudson then read us a bit of description about a hare bounding and gambolling on the hills and asked us to write a poem called The Mad March Hare, after she'd explained that they were called that because they sometimes got a bit hyperactive in spring. She asked if anybody knew what hyperactive meant and Noel Marsden said it meant you were active in the sky, and Mrs Hudson told us to get on with our work.

I enjoyed writing the poem and when I'd nearly finished it I took it to show Mrs Hudson, hoping she'd like it and that the greatness of the literary work would make her and me forget the rabbit/hare error I'd made earlier. Then, as now, I always wanted to be right. She told me she liked the poem but pointed out, very gently, that I'd spelled 'hare' as 'hair'. Mad March hair. I tried to smile but I felt the tears prickling my eyes. Double humiliation in one day.

I was thinking about that day the other morning when I wandered down the street to the paper shop; it was a typical breezy March day, the wind lifting a crisp bag in front of me and trying to hurl it into my face. A man strode by me in the other direction, attempting to hold his cap on and I realised, all these years later, that I'd been right all along in Mrs Hudson's class. It was mad March hair all the time.

The bloke's cap finally blew off and rolled down the street like a Frisbee with Brylcreem stains; his combover

danced like a lariat in a John Wayne film and he tried to retrieve the cap and tame the combover at the same time as though he was a juggler trying to eat fire. I leaped to grab the rolling cap and as I did I noticed a woman across the road holding her headscarf tight over her shellacked perm. My own quiff was doing a kind of primitive dance of the sort you associate with prog-loving sixth form boys at school discos in the 1970s.

The man's combover proved untameable and it waved and writhed in the manner of an octopus that had had far too many energy drinks. Another passerby stopped to help but his fringe was lifted by the gale like Marilyn Monroe's skirt and he couldn't see a thing and he flapped around blindly, trying in vain to tame the fringe's excesses. The three of us resembled that famous photograph of the US Marines raising the flag at Iwo Jima but with a flat cap instead of the flag. A flat cap that none of us could grab.

A bus pulled up and a bunch of passengers got off and all their different hairstyles were slapped and, indeed, tickled by the wild March wind. A short-back-and-sides ruffled like nervous suede. A Mohican bent to one side scarily, as though it might topple and flatten the owner's poodle. A couple of lads with Justin Bieber hair-alikes almost wept when their styles exploded and were left mortally wounded on their heads. Carefully patted and brushed barnets were reduced to anarchy.

I finally grabbed the man's cap and gave it back to him.

'Mad March hair, eh?' I said, triumphantly. 'You're right there, kid!' he said.

So there, Mrs Hudson. Where's my star?

When I was a boy it was always around late spring when my mam would take me to the shop to buy some new shorts; I wore short trousers all the time, of course, but these were special. They were my summer shorts. We'd get to the shop and I'd be struck rigid with embarrassment as my mam said, in a voice that was only slightly muffled by the racks of clothes and the silent assistants gliding around as if on castors, 'Right, it's time for my lad to get some shorts and then he can spend the summer showing off his PROPER YORKSHIRE KNEES!'

I put Proper Yorkshire Knees in capital letters there because that's how she said it, loudly, so that not only the people in the shop in Barnsley heard, but the ones in the Wakefield branch did too. My mam would then point at my knees and yell 'Look at them PROPER YORKSHIRE KNEES! Just look at 'em! Bring him some lovely shorts so he can show 'em off!' and I would glow like a tomato and wish that the ground would not only open up and swallow me, but would also transport me to a planet where nobody had knees.

Then, for the whole summer, I'd wear my shorts, which was fun. What wasn't fun was my mam's constant hymn of praise to my knees. 'Them's knees!' she'd say to any mates who happened to pop by, 'but them's just not any knees, them's … (and here we could all join in but we never did because we'd have got a scutch round the ear) PROPER YORKSHIRE KNEES!'

I tolerated it though, because well, I was ten and she was my mam. But then, the year after, I was, of course, eleven. I was, not to put too fine a point on it, starting to change,

to mature. My voice was beginning to break and little scrubby hairs were appearing on my top lip. I was starting to have complex protective feelings for Emma Peel on The Avengers and I wasn't sure why.

By that spring I was wearing long trousers because that's what Big Boys did so when my mam approached and carolled, 'It's time to get them PROPER YORKSHIRE KNEES out!' I ran and hid behind the shed. My mam wasn't to be put off. She trailed me like a knee-seeking device and found me cowering behind a pile of sticks. I tried to be reasonable although it's hard to be reasonable and cower at the same time. It didn't help that my voice ran up and down the scales like somebody's first viola lesson.

'Mam, I don't want to wear shorts any more. None of the lads are wearing shorts. Shorts are for little uns, and I'm not a little un anymore. Mam, please. Please: no shorts.' Mam was momentarily taken aback, mainly by the very odd sound of my voice as much as by what I was saying, but recovered quickly.

'No,' she said, her voice beginning to tremble, 'you've got to get some shorts. It's that time of year. You've got to show off your PROPER YORKSHIRE KNEES!' and her voice rose to a shrill crescendo so that I understood the gravity of what I was saying. Getting my knees out into the air was a ritual that was as much a part of the calendar as Christmas and Easter and Bonfire Night. If I refused the invitation to get some air on my PROPER YORKSHIRE KNEES then it would be as though a meteor of tradition had fallen, never to be extinguished.

So I went to the shop, my eyes red with weeping, my mouth hurting with turning it down in a full sulk. We went upstairs to where the shorts were, and there they were. But not only the shorts: my mates, all of them, with their mams. And buying shorts, all of them. And all the mams stood as one and shouted 'Let's see them PROPER YORKSHIRE KNEES!' as though some semblance of order had been restored to Yorkshire and the world. As perhaps it had.

I was thinking the other day about that old poem called November, by Thomas Hood; I remember reading it at Low Valley Junior School in Darfield on a dreary November day many decades ago and it was obviously memorable

because it's stuck with me. Or perhaps it's memorable because Mrs Hudson wouldn't let us have our milk until we'd learned it. You know the poem I mean: it starts 'No sun, no Moon,/ No morn, No noon/No dawn, no dusk, no proper time of day' and ends '…no fruits, no flowers, no trees, no birds — /November!'.

As I sat there musing on the truth of those words (with the light on, because it was dull outside) I began to formulate a Yorkshire response to Hood's famous lines, and I started to imagine them as spoken by somebody from

Leeds or Harrogate or Selby or Rotherham. I tried to make up a Yorkshire verse for the month that's only useful because it takes us up to the foothills of Christmas and lets us set off things that go bang and whizz in its very first week. Then I decided that I didn't need a verse and I went on the hunt for a single word that would crystallise the month for all time by renaming it in Yorkshire-ese.

If I'd been in an advertising agency or a branding consultancy (although I thought you only saw the latter in cowboy films, run by a dude called Zeke who had his own irons and his own fire) I'd have had a meeting in an office with some people in trendy shirts and thick-rimmed glasses and hair that sloped like some Sunday League football pitches do. We'd have chucked ideas around the table and stuck multicoloured Post-it notes to a board and shouted out things like 'let's just run with this one!' and 'stick with me for a few minutes here because I think this concept might have legs!' but no matter how long we chattered in that Post-it-bedecked room we wouldn't have come up with an idea as good as the one I just had: Nowtvember.

Let me write it again while you take it in: Nowtvember. Or, if you want to play with the font, NowtVember. Say it and a chill runs down your spine and you can see your breath and if you're wearing a muffler you tighten it and if you're not wearing a muffler you go and get one and put it on.

In one word, in my humble opinion, NowtVember (I prefer it with the capital V) sums up everything that Thomas Hood was trying to say in all those lines. With typical Yorkshire gruffness/dourness we've pinned down an unloved month in three syllables. I mean, look around; look at November. What is there to recommend it? Nowt. It's dark when you get up and dark when you go to bed. Mind you, that happened to my Uncle Jack in summer when he put his balaclava on back to front. The trees are bare. You can't see the church clock for the mist so you miss your bus. The cold penetrates as many layers as you care to put on and a few more besides. If the sun comes out it's like a child's drawing of the sun that only stays in the sky long enough to get covered by a cloud the colour of an old and unloved tea-towel. The one with a picture of clouds on it.

NowtVember: not so much a month, just a pile of unlovely days stacked up like out-of-date beans in a supermarket. NowtVember: less a month, more an irritation. NowtVember: if it was a window it would be a mucky one that you couldn't see through.

I'll tell you what: roll on December.

In February, when I was a lad, our house would reverberate to the sound of clicking; it wasn't that my dad, tiring of fly-fishing, was taking up playing the castanets; no, my mother would be knitting. Winter was always a good time for her to knit in front of the telly, and you could tell what she was watching by the speed of the knitting. She'd go like the clappers during a stampede on Wagon Train and she'd knit slowly and peacefully during a nature programme about the migration of reindeer across the Arctic tundra.

In fact, if you walked up our street on a quiet evening

you'd hear the rattling sound of mass knitting as, in their separate houses, Mrs Marsden and Mrs Page and Mrs White and Miss Hirst churned out scarves and jumpers and bootees like they were doing so for a bet.

And so it was inevitable that, in February 1965 at the age of nine, I thought I'd have a go at learning to knit. My Uncle Don enjoyed knitting and I felt, like him, that knitting shouldn't be the domain of the women of the family so I asked my mam if I could have a go at something simple. She plucked out a pattern for a scarf (the photograph on the front looked like James Bond's stunt double) and patiently gave me instructions on something that, for her, was more or less instinctive.

Like most males of the species I ignored the instructions which involved words like 'under' and 'over' and 'off' and just began. After all, how hard could it be? You just clicked for a bit and an item of clothing appeared. It wasn't brain surgery, unless you were knitting a brain. I got some wool on the end of one needle and attempted to make it connect with the other needle. It was as though I was eating soup with chopsticks. I began to sweat and get very irritated. I may have gone sunset-red. 'Have you dropped a stitch?' my mother asked, kindly. I nodded and she started me off again.

And I just couldn't do it. The wool got wrapped around my hands like manacles and then somehow the wool also got wrapped around the chair I was sitting in, finding its way beneath and across the cushion in a way that seemed to defy the laws of physics, or at least the laws of physics as we understood them in Yorkshire. I was like a boy enveloped in a spider's web in a cheap horror film. The cat came up and began to play with some of the wool that was trailing around the leg of the table I was sitting near and eventually got so entangled in the wool that it looked like a knitted cat.

I went puce with frustration. I didn't know what I was doing wrong (let's face it: I didn't know what I was doing at all) but I thought that if I did it more quickly all would be well. All was not well. All was the opposite of well. All was ill. My needles moved like I was in a speeded-up cartoon. The wool almost caught fire. I was dripping with sweat and my arms hurt. I began to cry. I tried to wipe my eyes and accidentally rubbed them with wool, making them itch and smart. I said 'stupid wool!' and my dad, trying to make light of the situation but failing miserably, said

'A bad workman blames his tools' and even though he said it with a chuckle in his voice it tipped me over the edge into a full-blown nine-year-old-boy's tantrum and I began to shout things that I now regret. I shouted ridiculous and embarrassing phrases like 'It's the wool's fault! These needles are bent! I don't want a scarf anyway, I want to knit something else like a coat!'.

I flung a needle in the air and it landed on the cat which ran into the kitchen. I stormed from the room, if you can storm from a room when you're mummified by wool. I shouted from the kitchen, 'I don't want to do knitting any more! I want to try crochet!' My mam carried on knitting and my dad turned the telly up.

We all know the old saying 'Ne'er cast a clout 'til May is out' meaning, in Yorkshire-speak, it's best to keep your muffler on until after the Whit holidays. When I was younger and more impressionable I thought the saying was a call for World Peace, or at least World Peace Until Late Spring, which isn't quite the same thing. I thought 'casting a clout' meant giving somebody a clip round the ear or a stiff blow to the solar-plexus, and I thought the wise old saw was calling for pacifism until the nights really started drawing out.

Indeed, I remember once, after somebody at school had gently punched me in the nose, shouting 'Mrs Hudson! Robert's cast a clout at me!' I was baffled by her reply, which was, 'Well, use it to mop up that spilled paint.'

Recently I found a diary I kept as a teenager once I'd discovered the real meaning of the phrase; it was supposed

to follow, in detail, my adventures in clout-casting, but as I re-read I realised it was a hymn to the uncertainty of Yorkshire weather and the exuberant stupidity of adolescence. Here's an extract:

Monday: warm day. Cast clout. Mam gave me a clout (different kind) and said something about not leaving my scarves around the place. I assured her that I was in the middle of a clout-casting social experiment and she pointed out that we were only halfway through May so no clouts should be cast anyway. I replied that the temperature was high and I couldn't possibly keep my clout on until the end of the month, and we left the conversation at that impasse. Went outside: chilly. Went back inside, retrieved clout. Walked down street with clout in place. Got a bit of a sweat on. Went into pub, cast clout. Mates in pub asked what I was doing and then parodied me by casting beer-mats and bar towels around until the landlord told us to stop or he'd set the husky on us. None of us believed he'd really got a husky but none of us wanted to find out. One of my mates asked him if the husky was called Clout but got no reply. Went home.

Tuesday: Cold day. Went out for a stroll with clout firmly attached. Sun burst through a cloud. Day warmed up. Neck began to glow, then perspire, then sweat. Refused to cast clout because, in the spirit of the experiment, there were still several days to go until the end of May. Felt dizzy and unstable with heat. Finally cast clout to prevent collapse and possible hospitalisation. Sun went in. Clout on. Sun out. Clout cast. Sun in again. Clout on again. Sun out again. Clout cast again. One of my mates watching from across the road said it looked like I was performing a folk dance from the Ossett Vortex. I waved my clout aggressively but he only laughed.

Wednesday: Freezing, even in the house. Wore clout in the bathroom as I did my teeth; wore it in the kitchen as the kettle boiled. Sat around all day in the clout then went to bed, still in the clout. Neck itched terribly as though thousands of Hetton-le-Hole Commando Ants were nibbling their way through to my Adam's apple. Cast clout. Checked in mirror and where the clout had been there was a phantom clout, a red line that etched its way round my neck like one of those tattoos that says CUT HERE.

Thursday: Decided to see how far I could actually cast the clout, trying to remove it and cast it in one swift movement. Stood in the garden, whirling like a shot-putter. Cast the clout, cricking my neck and causing me great pain. Sank to my knees. Watched as the cast clout whirled through the sky like a gull. Cursed the clout. Cursed weather-based folklore. Next door neighbour threw the clout back and it landed on my head. I cast it to the ground. I stamped on it. I attempted to tear it up. My neck really, really hurt. Diary ends here.

When I was about nine my dad decided it was time I learned to ride a bike; when I asked him why, he said 'It's just something lads your age should do' and when I replied that I was happy enough with my Biggles books and the comfortable and capacious settee, he launched into a flight of fancy that was half reverie, half tone-poem,

I could have been a contender...

about the carefree days of his childhood when he cycled to school and cycled home from school and then cycled all evening with the wind streaming through his hair until the sun went down. I tried to imagine my dad with enough hair for the wind to stream through but gave it up as a bad job. 'My mum said if I spent any longer in the saddle I'd turn into a bike,' he said. 'Bad news,' I replied, 'you have.' He didn't get it.

I was prised from the settee with the promise of some Yorkshire Mixtures and we went to the house of a bloke in the next village who advertised second-hand bikes in the local paper. I'd recently seen Oliver Twist on TV and this feller's back room reminded me of Fagin's Den: as we went in and stood at the very edge of the dingily lit space wringing our hands and looking nervous and feeling out of place, a number of urchins nipped in and out, each one thinner and more ferret-faced than the last. I gazed at them in wonder, thinking they were all related somehow, but later my dad said they were just, in his words, 'ruffians from down near the football ground' and the stuff they were offering the bike bloke was probably stolen.

The bicycle entrepreneur sat on a chipped kitchen chair, or rather he enveloped it, his huge belly sticking out like a beach ball, his hair blossoming from his head at all angles as though it had been discovered at the bottom of the sea and brought to the surface and spread out to dry. A mucky-looking kid came in with a bicycle bell. 'Giz a shilling for it,' he said. 'Ring it first,' said the bloke. It rang with a cracked and pleading tone, the man threw a tanner across the room and his supplier scuttled off into the night.

The bloke looked at me and my dad. 'Can I help yer?' he wheezed, the breath making a supreme effort to leave his body and then get dragged back in, his voice as squeaky as a first recorder lesson. 'We'd like a bike,' my dad said, unnecessarily. The man waved his hand around the kitchen. 'Take your pick,' he piped. An Artful Dodger offered to show us round, his grin revealing teeth like torn cardboard.

And that's how I ended up at the bottom of our garden, my dad holding the back of a bike that was slightly too big for me and me hanging onto the handlebars as though they were a lifeboat and the lawn was an ocean churning and boiling in a Force 10 gale. 'Pedal!' my dad shouted in what novelists call 'an exasperated tone' and I tried, I really did, I promise I did. I went forward about two yards simply because my dad had let go of the bike and shoved me in the back and then I collapsed in a pile that was part boy, part handlebars, part lawn, part pedals, part garden path, part tyres and part weeping. My dad, a kindly man, seemed to be at the end of his tether. 'Let's go in and get some milk,' he said. 'And can I finish my Biggles book?' I sobbed. He nodded.

The next day we took the bike back to the wheezing chap-mountain and he gave us five pounds less than we'd paid for it and it was never mentioned again.

And that's why I have great admiration for all the competitors in those cycling races around Yorkshire. Good luck to you all. And here's a bit of sage advice from One Who Knows: Pedal. Except when you don't need to.

Trick or treat or sudden death...

In the 1960s when I was growing up, I seem to remember that we made quite a lot of Halloween in Yorkshire; we'd carve turnip lanterns at school and make witches' hats from cardboard and coloured paper and giant spider's webs from bits of string; Mrs Roche would tell us scary stories in the Story Corner, pausing theatrically in the narrative just before she made us jump, pausing for so long that we thought she wouldn't make us jump, but she always made us jump anyway, and we loved it.

The one thing we didn't do was go out trick-or-treating because most of us had only a vague idea about what it was, and all we knew was that in no way could it have been as exciting and terrifying as Mrs Roche's stories. As the 1960s began to age and decay, though, and the 1970s waited round the corner with all their newness and modernity, me and my mates were becoming more and more aware of trick-or-treat because we read American comics and we watched American films and TV series and it seemed like an easy way to make money. From what we could work out from our Batman and Superman comics and I Love Lucy on the TV, you just went to somebody's house, said 'Trick or Treat?' and people gave you money. It felt like easy cash to us, easy cash to take to Wombwell market to buy more comics.

So me and Chris and Martin resolved to go trick-or-treating on Halloween. We couldn't really work out what the 'trick' in 'trick-or-treat' was, but we'd seen people on American sitcoms get cross when the trick-or-treaters, having been refused a treat, fired a catapult through a window, much to the consternation of the man next door. Me and the lads thought this might be a bit drastic so we decided to just threaten to use the catapult. That would be enough of a trick, we reckoned, for a first go.

We popped round to Mr and Mrs White, who lived next door to us; we stood outside their back door debating who should knock; we could hear their radio in the back room and Mr and Mrs White singing along to hymns. In the end our debating led nowhere so, after a few games of Scissors/Paper/Stone, I had to knock. I knocked as loudly as I could, which still took a while to penetrate the Wesleyan Wall of Sound.

After several minutes I heard Mr White say 'There's

somebody at the door' and Mrs White reply 'I bet it's the stick man. Tell him we don't want any. I've enough sticks to start a wood.' The television was switched off.

Mr White opened the door and the three of us said 'Trick or Treat?' in unison. Mr White looked baffled. 'You what?' he said. 'Is it the stick man?' Mrs White shouted. 'No,' Mr White said, 'It's Ian from next door with his mates asking if we've got a wicker seat.' Mrs White bustled in and looked at us sceptically. 'What do you want a wicker seat for?' she asked. 'Trick or treat?' we said again, like people in a new country trying out a new phrase from a book.

'Who?' said Mrs White. 'Nobody of that name here; there's only me and Mr White.' Chris stepped forward; he was impulsive and his patience was wearing thin. 'Trick or treat or else we'll catapult thi!' he said, his voice breaking with menace and the approach of puberty. 'Cat's out,' said Mr White. I'd never noticed before that they were deaf; it only occurred to me years later that they weren't deaf at all and they knew what they were doing all along.

We made one last concerted effort and bellowed 'Trick or Treat?' Mrs White gazed at us and said 'Treat. You can now give me and Mr White a treat.' We were baffled. 'That's not how it works!' I whined. 'It is in Yorkshire!' Mr White said, grabbing and pocketing the chocolate bar I was holding. That was our last attempt at trick-or-treat for a while, I can tell you.

Lessons for life

Well, just look who's here: 2016, coming in the door like an unexpected guest, like the rent man, like the uncle coming home from Australia where he flew to in 1964 as a ten pound Pom from Rotherham. How on earth can it be 2016? The last time I looked it was, well, about 2002, or if you look at my haircut it could still be the late 1950s, my greying quiff sprouting like the winner of last year's Skipton Elvis Topiary Festival.

Time, eh? Who can fathom it? How can you turn round as a 25-year-old with 20/20 vision and then the next time you look, or try to, you're a granddad with glasses on who tells the kids to turn their music down? And, of course, nothing exemplifies and demonstrates and encapsulates the passage of time for the Yorkshire person like the Yorkshire pudding: it's our diary, our calendar, our almanac and our St Paul's Cathedral and our Stonehenge.

Think about it. You start off with the idea, the thought: I'll make a Yorkshire pudding. You don't need a recipe because the recipe's in your head, planted there either by your parents or by the very fact of living in Yorkshire. You get the flour, you get the eggs, you get the milk. In my case, you get the pepper, because I like a peppery Yorkshire. And that's another fact about the Yorkshire pudding: everybody makes it in their own way. It's like a jazz solo that takes a tune and makes variations on it.

And, like a jazz solo, it's an exercise in the manipulation of time.

You glance at the clock. The joint's in the oven. The veg are ready and waiting in the pan. You calculate how long it will take to mix the Yorkshires and you divide that by the time it will take the oven to get hot enough without burning the joint, and you subtract the mixing time and you work out to the exact second just when you should be whipping the batter into a frenzy.

You begin to mix. History and Time and Tradition lean over your shoulder as you twirl the tines: all the Yorkshire people who ever made Yorkshire puddings are standing behind you in a queue and every time your hand moves the fork you're demonstrating the glory of Yorkshire evolution. From amphibious creatures in the ooze of the Ouse to the Yorkshire pudding chef: what a glorious piece of

work the human being is. The mixture is ready and you pop it in the oven, and then after an always variable but always perfect length of time, the alchemy has happened and the mixture has risen to heaven and turned a glorious brown and the pudding is done.

So let's make 2016 the year of the real Yorkshire pudding. Let's banish those fake ones (you know the ones I mean) to the recycling dump of history. Let's demand the real deal in pubs and restaurants. We don't mind waiting; we know that there's no such thing as an instant Yorkshire pudding, and that Yorkshire puddings are examples of slow food at its very very best.

Let's remind that Ten Pound Pom just why he wanted to come home to Rotherham, because you just can't make the batter rise in WurraBurra!

I've always been a chap who wakes up early, my eyes clanging open sometime just before 5am when some people in nightclubs are debating whether or not to have one for the road and trying to locate their house keys. Perhaps I'm just built that way, or perhaps I've inherited wakefulness from my dad because he spent decades in the Royal Navy on the four-hour watch, always getting up and standing to attention and slipping on his hat four hours after he went to bed, even when he'd left the navy and had nothing to watch except Bonanza.

I also put part of my larkiness down to the late great Colin Leech, conductor of the Thurnscoe Harmonic Male Voice Choir. It wasn't that he woke me up with his singing: no, he woke me up with his whirring and clinking, because as well as being a superb musical leader he was also a milkman.

I've lived in the same house near Barnsley for more than twenty years and, for the first ten years or so, each morning just before five I'd be harmonically pulled from the Land of Nod by the musical drone of Colin's milkfloat and the glass bells of his semi-skimmed and full fat. Colin retired and the new milkman trundled down the street much later in the day in a float which hummed a different note but the Leech alarm still rang in my head. And at this time of year I don't mind waking up early because I can tell, by the slight alteration in the darkness beyond the window and

Ian's heart stopped... Oh no, he groaned, my wife's favourite Gnome

the tentative peep of a bird somewhere in the big trees by the cemetery, that spring is on its way.

March really does open the door to spring and, if you look carefully across the landscape at that time of year you can see summer loitering in the wings. This month is the month the year really comes to life; I get up in March and I walk down to the paper shop and sometimes I can still see my breath, and sometimes I need my scarf and my hat, but it's still spring. The Yorkshire sky is the brightest, freshest blue and the vapour trails of the planes are like new white paint on a stretched canvas. People who previously nodded to you from beneath their pulled brims now say the full 'Good Morning' and they grin, teeth almost as white as a vapour trail in the sky. Almost.

And it's in March that my wife's thoughts turn to the garden and this year I'm determined that I'm going to join her. When we first moved to this house I offered to help with some weeding because I'd been awake since ten to five and up since half past; she pointed out the area I could work in and left me to it — which was a mistake, because I ripped out something that looked like a weed but was in fact a plant she'd just spent a lot of money on at the garden centre. I pathetically tried to dig the destroyed blooms back in, but that was the end of me in the garden for that decade. In fact, for that century, and that millennium. This year, though, is going to be my year. I'm going to be the Lt Cdr J McMillan RN of the soil, always on the watch for what's a weed and what isn't; I'll be the Colin Leech of the shrubs, spreading harmony from the lawn to the shed, from the little bench to the apple tree. I'll be the king of the garden, the Alan Titchmarsh of the South Yorkshire Coalfield, the jolly green-fingered giant who knows a weed from a flower blindfold.

I'll start in a small way, though. I'll fetch and I'll carry. I'll bring her trowel to her when she needs it. I'll dig only where directed. I'll push the barrow to the compost heap. I'll wash the plantpots. The spring sunshine will warm me up and I'll go to bed pleasantly tired with the feeling that, at last, I'm a gardener. Then I'll wake up at five to five and rush downstairs to read the backs of seed packets in the kitchen as the kettle boils. Spring, you see: it gets in your bones.

I'll be with you in a minute. Just a minute. I'm just about to write a hymn of praise to the glory that is a Yorkshire August but I can't get on with it because of this flipping fly. I bet if you hold your ear close to the page you'll be able to hear it; it's buzzing around my head, diving close to my keyboard like a small plane spraying a field. It's been in the room since I made the mistake of leaving the door open and it wandered in like the Rent Man. There it goes again. Get out! Get away!

Sorry. I'm back. I just chased the fly across the room with a rolled up copy of *Dalesman*; I wish you could have seen me, in my summer polo shirt and my shorts, running across the carpet like a Tyke version of Hermes the Winged Messenger of the Gods. Don't know if old Hermes wore a polo shirt and shorts but if he did he'd have looked like me. If he had glasses on. If he was unshaven. If he was shouting GERRRRAAAT YER

THING! to a fly. I wielded my copy of *Dalesman* like a club and I think I might have got it. I might have stunned it, wounded it, showed it that you don't mess about with a Yorkshireman. Especially a Yorkshireman in shorts and slippers. Right. Back to it. The Yorkshire August: a time of lazy summer days. A time of strolls along the beach at Scarborough or a time to have an ice cream in the main square in Grassington or a time to spread your picnic rug on the grass and get out the sandwiches and the pop and ...get attacked by a fly. It's back.

Let me at it with this hardback copy of *Yorkshire Humour* by me and Tony Husband. It's a hilarious book but not if you're a fly. I'm windmilling my arms around,

slashing the air with *Yorkshire Humour* and I'm sure the fly is taunting me, teasing me, swooping close to my face and then darting away.

I reckon it's not any old fly. I reckon this is the Fly of Doom. I reckon this is the Fly of Passing Time, reminding me that in August's heat is the promise of autumn, of September and October and November and the run-in to Christmas and the harsh months that follow. I've written before about the melancholy I feel in August, the idea that summer is almost over, and this fly is reminding me of the turning of the seasons. Well it won't be reminding me for much longer. Take that!

Flipping heck: I missed the fly and hit my cup of tea, sending it spiralling into the air like the wine glasses on the Titanic. Tea all over. Soaking tablecloth. A brown river heading across the table. Blooming fly. Look how it buzzes serenely round the room, looking at Hermes the Winged God mopping up the tea. If a fly could laugh, then this one's laughing.

Right. Back to it. Yorkshire in August: donkey rides, paddling pools in the garden, white flat caps and thin summer cardigans and ...I've just realised. I get it now. The fly isn't the Fly of Doom, isn't even the Fly of Passing Time. Listen to the buzzing. Listen to the faint upward note at the end of each buzzing phrase. Listen to the tone of the buzz.

It's a Lancashire Fly. Listen to the faint Bolton or Blackburn tinge to the buzz. A Lancashire Fly. No wonder it's cross. It woke up on a sunny day in Lancashire and through a mixture of thermals and stiff breezes and slight winds and sudden squalls, and being caught in the slip-stream of a double-decker bus, and being carried for a short distance by a bird and then dropped, it's ended up here, in Yorkshire.

No wonder it's cross. It was expecting to land on some Lancashire hotpot and instead it's going to land on some Yorkshire pudding. I'll take a risk. I'll open the door a crack and try to waft it out and then it can fly back to Lancashire. There: open the door a little way and ...there it goes. Bye-bye Mr Lancashire Fly, as Don McLean almost sang.

That's better. A fresh cup of tea and a column to write. Yorkshire in August. Oh no: I've left the front door open. He's back. And he's brought his mates ....

Now then, old pal. Just keep reading this page. Don't look up. Don't shout to t' wife or t' husband. Just keep looking at the page. There's nothing wrong. Nothing's going to happen to you if you just keep looking at the page. This is no ordinary book, you see. This one is a special edition. And you've been chosen.

Let me explain. Just keep looking at the page. Don't try and put me back, don't try and look at any other copies to see if they're all like this. They aren't. This is unique. And there's nothing to worry about. Nothing at all. You're about to become a very rich man, a very rich man indeed. You remember Yorkshire Gold? You must remember that? That breezeblock-sized slab of pure gold mined and refined from the Giggleswick gold mines and then buried in a secret spot in 1966 in a blaze of publicity to be dug up fifty years later? Well those fifty years are up. Today. And you're the chosen one. Yes, it's you. All your birthdays have come at once, my friend. That gold breezeblock is worth millions in today's money. Millions. You'll never have to work again. You can eat as many pork pies as you like. You can have special giant pork pies made that you can ride about in. If you like pork pies, that is. It's just an example. You might like brown sauce sandwiches: bring 'em on!

Right, here's what you do. If you've bought this book in a shop, go out of the shop. If you've had it delivered, walk out of your house. Either is okay. Turn left. Walk for

If tha doesn't come down now, I'll give tha Yorkshire pud to the dog!

about half a mile, straight on, or as straight as you can. Stop. In front of you you'll see a tree. Yes, you're amazed, aren't you? Now, some people might think that the gold is buried under the tree but it isn't. It's not that simple. We're going to make you work for this obscene wealth. Climb the tree. Go on, climb the tree. Take your time. No rush. Don't worry about feeling daft climbing a tree with a copy of this book in your hand. Those people laughing at you from the bottom of the tree aren't about to become millionaires, are they? No.

Now you're at the top of the tree. Hold tight. Now, look to your right. You can see a man, can't you? Over there. Yes, that's right. He's going to lead you to the Breezeblock of Gold. You need to shout to him. As loud as you can because he's a long way away. Shout these words: 'You are Flat Cap Frankie and I claim my large piece of gold!'. Go on, do it. Don't be embarrassed. Don't worry that a large crowd has gathered and a stout copper is pushing his way through the crowd. Just keep shouting 'You are Flat Cap Frankie and I claim my large piece of gold!'.

Louder. Shout louder. What? He's taking no notice? And he's not wearing a cap? Why didn't you say so? Must be the wrong bloke. Must be the wrong tree. Okay, start again. Go back to your house or go back to the shop. You must have to turn right, not left. I could have sworn it was left. Don't tell me I've forgotten where we've buried the gold. I knew I should have written it down. Anyway, go back to where you set off from and we'll start again. Don't forget: you're about to become a very rich man ....

I'm still shaking, reader. I'm all of a dither. If you could see me writing this at a table in a café in a small North Yorkshire town you'd note that I don't look my usual cheerful self. I'm pale. My eyes are red as though I've recently been blubbering. My breath is laboured and just on the edge of a sob. The trademark McMillan thumb is not raised. Doctors might say that I'm in shock. Unless they were Doctors of Philosophy of course, in which case they'd dispute whether I was sitting at a table at all, since a 'table' is simply a 'table-shaped thing' that we choose to call a 'table'. Well, believe me, as I 'write' this, the very heart of my 'existence' has been called into question, in a philosophical 'way'.

Let me explain. Beside me there's a book, an innocent-looking book with a dark, shabby cover. I picked it up in a charity shop about half an hour ago when I was looking through the paperbacks for that lost Biggles novel, *Biggles Goes to Halifax*. I was intrigued by the title: *Jasper Hoopthorpe's Lancashire Japes*, first published in 1834. Although I am, of course, first and foremost a cultural historian of the Ridings, I do occasionally like to see what our mates over t' hill have been getting up to. Reader, I wish I'd never picked the book up. I WISH I'D NEVER PICKED THE BOOK UP! Sorry. Sorry. I didn't mean to shout.

The book was fairly normal Lancashire fare for the most part, with Hoopthorpe's mundane japes including 'Going to the Foot of My Stairs' and 'Hot Foot with a Hot Pot', but towards the end of the volume I discovered a small paragraph that is the cause of my café-table distress. It was entitled 'Foolin' Th' Yorkies i' Song', and it revealed that

the Yorkshire Anthem, 'Ilkley Moor Baht 'At', that hymn to lugubriousness, regeneration and the chewing of ducks, was in fact penned by the aforementioned Hoopthorpe, a lifelong resident of Clitheroe. He explains: 'I allus like to put one over on th' Yorkies who allus reckin they're superior fowk i' matters o' music.'

He goes on to describe how, with the aid of some friends from Blackburn, Darwen and Bolton he penned the song, inscribed it on some parchment and distributed it around the Ilkley area. The song was soon taken up as the song of Yorkshire's Founding Myth and the rest, as they say, is history. Or, as our Doctors of Philosophy would say, 'history' because, as I've just discovered and you're now discovering, the song is a lie. It's hard to imagine the sheer devastating importance of the news to a proud Yorkshire-man like me. My tea is going cold in its cup. It's like finding out that the world is triangular or that Santa Claus is a woman from Hartlepool. The whole edifice of my York-shireness, of all our Yorkshirenesses, is crumbling. I'm sorry to bring the readers of this book such bad news.

I know what I need to do; obviously the act I'm about to perform is a piece of artistic vandalism of the highest order and I would never even contemplate it in any other circumstances but the integrity of the White Rose is at stake. It's like an American finding out that a Canadian wrote the Star Spangled Banner. I need to destroy the book, to burn it or tear it up. Ah, but what good will that do? There will be other copies. The truth will out. Good-bye, Ilkley Moor Baht 'At: you may as well be Lassie from Lancasheer.

Ah well, at least we've still got the Yorkshire pudding. Wait a minute: what's this little article right at the back of the book. 'How the Yorkshire pudding was invented in Accrington ...'. Nooo!

I wake up at what my wife calls 'pit time', somewhere in that unmapped and mysterious region between half-past four and five o'clock when some people are still coming home from the night before and most people are snoring gently and one or two people are counting sheep and trying to snatch a bit of zizz before the alarm.

I get up. I wander downstairs. There's something in the air and it's not the miasma from my slipper-socks. I get dressed and go for my morning constitutional. I can tell that something's a little different, that Yorkshire (and maybe the rest of the world, but who really cares about the rest of the world?) has shifted a little since yesterday. I walk briskly down the street; I do this version of power-walking every morning in the naive belief that it holds back the advancing years. Well, it's either power-walking or plastic surgery and I'd look daft with a smooth face. I'd look like Humpty Dumpty with glasses on.

I look down. I appear to be on fire. The power-walking has caused me to spontaneously combust. No, it's not smoke. It's my breath. You can see my breath rising into the air as I walk. That's the change I half-detected. Even though it's still August and the schools are still on holiday and I'm still wearing my shorts around the house and firing up the barbecue every now and then, I'm sorry to say that summer's almost over.

I gaze at the tree at the bottom of my street; phew, all the leaves are still green. Summer's hanging on, holding autumn back against the odds. Then my eye is taken by a leaf right at the far side of the tree and my heart sinks. The leaf is just beginning to turn from green to brown. It isn't brown yet, of course; in fact to the casual observer it's still green, But not to me: there's gravy in the mint sauce, if you get my drift.

I continue my power-walk with the corners of my mouth turned down; I'm sad. I don't want summer to be over. I want it to hang on, and on, and on. And then I have a thought. The kind of thought that only a daft Yorkshire-man like me could ever have: I'll keep summer alive and

deny the movement of time. I'll pretend it's always August. I'll be like those people who, on the Twelfth Day of Christmas, decide to leave their decorations up and have turkey every day and keep the Christmas tree in the lounge until all the needles have fallen off and got sucked into the Hoover. I used to think those 'always Yule' types were ridiculous examples of humanity who should, in the words of the kids on the street, 'get a life' but now I realise how wrong I was, and how right they were.

I'll be Mr Summer, wearing my flip-flops all year long, sitting in a deckchair in the garden in the snow, having shivery barbecues in the November mist. I'll try and persuade the rest of our road to join in, maybe the rest of the village. It'll become a county-wide movement and it could even morph into a marketing tactic: Come to Yorkshire: It's Always Summer, Tha Knows! Come to Yorkshire: Tha'll Nivver Need A Muffler! It might work. It keeps Old Father Time locked in his shed.

It's either that or ring the plastic surgeon.

Now, if you're the same age as me and you're reading this at the start of the month you'll be rushing about like, as Auntie Mary used to say, 'somebody not reyt'. You'll be clambering out of the car somewhere in Yorkshire as fast as your middle-aged legs can carry you. You'll be rushing across the car park and piling into the tea shop at a speed just below that of light. You'll flop into the chair and you'll order a pot of tea and a toasted teacake and you'll breathe a sigh of relief. There will be a low hum of conversation and the odd chuckle. You'll be happy. You'll be content.

If, on the other hand, you're reading this at the end of the month, you'll have a resigned smile on your face. You'll be sitting in the same teashop, but at a larger table. One of the seats round the table will be a highchair with a baby in it. As well as the pot of tea and the teacake you'll have some bottles of pop and some ice creams. The noise level in the café will be moderate to high, with the occasional scream and the odd muttered threat. You'll be happy, but in a different way. Anyway, there's not quite as much time to be happy. Where are the tissues? Something's got spilt.

Yes, July is the month when the schools break up for the long and much-deserved summer holiday, and the month when grey-haired people like me play second fiddle in the

leisure and heritage and historical sites of the county to families with children. Now, I'm not being grumpy about this: I'm not one of those who wishes that kids should be seen but not heard, and over the years I've been a doting dad and granddad, but all I'm saying is that the transition, when it comes, is too sudden and too startling – like a light being flicked on in a darkened room. One minute you're walking down the beach at Brid and there's just you and your wife and a flask and a rucksack and some healthy sarnies, and you're saying something like 'this is the life!', and the next minute the beach is a school playground and your healthy sarnies look really middle-aged, really healthy, really brown and worthy next to all those exciting bags of crisps.

Again, I'm not complaining, but I just want the arrival

of the holidays to be staggered, then the arrival of the little uns is more of a trickle than a flood.

Some could break up on a Monday, a couple of weeks before they normally do, some on a Tuesday, and so on, until after fourteen days nobody is left at school. It can be like the gradual adding of an ingredient to a recipe. If you put the sorrel in too fast it overwhelms the dish, just like the sudden arrival of eighty-three families can overwhelm any museum café. Let the holidays begin gradually, so that the young people can be absorbed slowly into the landscape; they can appear in ones and twos to start with, like swallows on a telephone wire, not all at once like a flock of starlings round a dropped pork pie.

In September when they've all gone, I miss them, though. One minute there they are and the next minute there they're not and they're all back in school working hard. And it's just you and your wife in the café with the tea and the toasted teacake. So maybe they should go back to school gradually, too, just to give us old uns time to adjust. I'll have a word with somebody … .

Here we are at a Yorkshire bus stop. Here we are at a Yorkshire railway station. Here we are at a motorway services somewhere on the map of Great Britain. Here we are at an airport somewhere in the world. And because this is August, all the aforementioned locations are full of people from the White Rose County, and because it's August and because they're from Yorkshire, they're having a Frank Exchange of Views. Okay, not to put too fine a point on it, they're arguing in the special way that only people from Yorkshire can; in other words both sides are right and both sides are wrong at the same time. And don't they know it. Let's eavesdrop and the words will be terribly familiar to us all and, to be honest, you can almost listen to them in any order and they'll still sound like a Yorkshire August Discussion:

Have you turned the gas off? No, because it's your job. I always turn the gas off so I decided it should be your turn this year. Why didn't you tell me? Because you always seem to know what I'm thinking anyway. You've not packed those trunks, have you? I like these trunks. I liked them as well, in 1976 when you bought them. I know they sag a bit, but they're comfortable. Sagging isn't the word:

226

they look like they're melting when you put them on. I like them, they keep me covered. Can I let you into a secret: they don't.

Can I just check the passports one more time? No. I know I've checked them fifteen times already but can I just check them once more? I just need to see that they're still there? No. I just need to put my hands on them to be completely certain that they're there. Can I just look at them, then? Can I just pick up the little bag they're in because I'll know by the weight of the little bag that we've packed them? No.

Have you got the teabags? Yes. Have you put the teabags in the bottom of the case? Yes. You know they can't make proper tea over there, so have you got the teabags? Will 400 be enough? Do you think we should take some more? No. I can wrap them in my thermal vest, I'm sure they won't burst. Yes, I know we're only going to Morecambe for the weekend but you can never be too careful as far as teabags go. Remember what happened to Uncle Derek?

Why do we always go to the same place every year? Why do we always go for the same week every year? Why do we always set off at the same time to go to the same place for the same week every year? Why do we always have to take your mam? Why can't her tortoise go into the tortoise kennels? Well, I reckon she loves that tortoise more than she loves me. She does. She told me the other day it moved faster than me and had better breath. She did! Are you listening to me?

I don't want to go camping. It's you that said you wanted to go camping. No, it's you that said you wanted to go camping. No, it's you that said you wanted to go camping. (As you've realised, this is a three-way argument.) Anyway, it's not camping, it's glamping. What's glamping? It's camping in a bigger tent with a bedside lamp. I don't like camping or glamping, I like roughing it. What's roughing it? It's glamping in a small tent with no bedside lamp. Well if none of us want to go camping or glamping or roughing it, why are we going to a campsite?

Why can't we just stay at home? Why can't we just sit in the garden and have a barbecue? Why can't we pretend we're in a posh hotel and put some cushions on the bed and a bit of bland art on the wall? Now you're being cynical: I've booked us into a nice hotel. I bet it's got cushions on the bed. Well, what if it has, you can always take them off. I bet it's got bland art on the wall. Well, what if it has: your pictures would give them nightmares. They wouldn't! They would. Roll on September.

I reckon that everybody in Yorkshire has got an ancient biscuit tin somewhere full of old black-and-white family photographs; they're all different, of course, because all families are different, but in the end, when you think about it properly, they might all just be variations on the same few topics.

There's always one of an unidentified baby lying on a rug; there's always a grandma in a hat smiling from the back window of a saloon car; there's always a bloke in a cap holding up a fish, and there's inevitably the most common one of all, the group in a staggered line wandering down a windy seafront and grinning at the lens.

In July in those days everybody would head to the seaside, either in cars or more often on packed trains, endlessly shunting in and out of places like Bridlington and Scarborough, disgorging people who were glad to be away from the mill or the pit or the steelworks, glad to get the sun on their backs and some good sea air in the lungs. 'It's like wine, this air!' they would say to each other, and nobody could tell what they were saying because their mouths were full of fish and chips and nobody would care.

I look at these 1960s pictures of my family and other families and I'm amazed at how formal they look: the men are often wearing suits and wide-brimmed hats and the women are wearing beautiful dresses or skirts and tops and they could be on their way to a wedding or the opera. In fact, they're just taking part in the theatre of the seaside. The wind flaps the trousers of their suits and threatens Marilyn Monroe moments for the women to shriek and laugh about later in the sewing factory on long autumn afternoons.

I was born in 1956 so I realise that what I'm describing here was almost dying out as I was growing up: the street photographers who would snap the strolling groups and who would ask them to come and pick up the prints at five o'clock by the pier, just before the trains and buses left for the other end of the county. I have a vague, vague memory of a man with a flying combover getting me and my mam and dad and my brother and Uncle Jack and Auntie Mary and cousin Josephine to stand still just for a moment while he took our picture; I remember him taking the snap, but I also recall how upset I got when we never picked it up, how we drove home from, I think, Scarborough, with me blubbering on the back seat because we didn't get the photo. The ones that were picked up and paid for are now in the biscuit tins and big brown envelopes and photo albums that help us to remember who we once were and maybe who we wanted to become.

And now older people are amazed that we seem to have developed (get it?) into a much more photographed race. To be photographed is not special any more. We are always taking pictures of each other on our phones and our tablets, and we send them to each other and we marvel at them for a moment and then we forget them and take another one. If I was a young lad now with all those other people walking along the front we'd pause for a moment and take a selfie, and we'd all crowd into it until we looked

like a shoal of fish at the edge of a tank. Some of us would put our thumbs up; some of us would make rabbit ears behind somebody else and somebody, like they always have ever since the first group photo was taken, would have their eyes shut.

And this is not a bad thing; I'm pleased that the screen has replaced the biscuit tin. I'm happy that my life and the lives of those around me are measured in photographs. I'm still a little sad, though, when I think of that old street photographer waiting forlornly for us to turn up and buy our snaps. I'm sorry, my friend. At least we all smiled and said 'Cheese!'.

I hope the next twelve months bring you everything you hope for, some surprises and at least one event that makes you go 'By gum, I never thought that was going to happen!'. Mind you, I know exactly what's going to happen to me this month: I'm going to turn sixty. I'm going to officially grow up, to reach maturity, to become a mature (if not senior) citizen and let me tell you I can't wait. I've been waiting for this moment all my life.

Let's face it, us Yorkshiremen are all born old. Childhood seems to pass us by like a fast train zooming up the line as a stopping pacer limps from station to halt to station. Look at Brian Blessed. Look at Brian Close. Look at J B Priestley. As infants they could have got served in pubs and as adolescents they looked ready to retire and once they got older they just looked extremely comfortable in their own skin. Well, I'm here at last; I've joined the throng of the fully-developed.

Come on, kids: respect me. I'm your elder and your better and I'm ready to receive your good wishes. Gifts are acceptable too, as long as they're the kinds of presents that sixty-year-old Tykes will appreciate, like pipes and beer tankards and (even though I can't drive) leather driving gloves with natty patterns of holes in the backs of the hands. I can now hold forth in pubs and bars without fear of being told to button it or, worse, ignored like I was when I was a young whippersnapper of fifty-nine. I'll be able to stand there and command silence by the very presence of my bright lapel badge that says '60 TODAY' as the sunlight bounces off my grey quiff.

Oh, the joy: I've just realised I'll be able to start every sentence with the fabled phrase 'When I were a lad ...' and nobody will object, and anyway if they do I'll be able to brandish my birth certificate and when they see I'm sixty they'll quieten down and listen with dewy eyes to my pearls of wisdom. I'll tell them that they don't know they're born. I'll tell them it used to be all fields round here. I'll tell them you could get three pints and a bag of crisps and have a bet on a horse and get your muffler dry-cleaned and still have change from a ten bob note. I'll sing 'Daisy, Daisy' and I'll be appalled when they don't know the words.

Hang on a minute, though. I'm only sixty. I'm not my dad. I'm not my granddad. I should be singing Sex Pistols songs to them, not First World War songs: punk was the sound of my youth when my grey quiff was a dark quiff that wanted to be a red Mohican.

And that's the odd thing about being a mature York-shireman and it goes back to the thing I said a few

Eeee...Your Ian's very much like his
Dad isn't he

paragraphs ago: Yorkshire blokes like being old, and when we're sixty we secretly think we're about seventy-five, even though we've been told that sixty is the new forty. I hope all these numbers aren't confusing you. They're confusing me but that's okay: I'm sixty and it's a long time since I was at school.

Ah, sixty: well, as far as us White Rose Lads are concerned, sixty is the new eighty. Not only can we spout hackneyed homilies and rusty saws, we can dress as sloppily as we like. Pass me my old cardigan, the one with more holes than wool. Hand me my slippers that cost £2 on the market when £2 was a lot of money. Pass me my shapeless jacket and my corduroy trousers. There: that's better. I look my age now. Or older, which is better.

And the flat cap. Of course, the flat cap. I reckon that,

even among us quickly-ageing Yorkshiremen, the flat cap can only really be worn once we get to sixty. Before that, we're wearing them with a tinge of irony, we're wearing them because, Heaven forbid, we think they're retro and trendy, or we're wearing them for a joke. Not any longer, boys and girls, not any longer.

The flat cap is placed firmly on the head. The slippers are so comfortable it's like I'm walking on air. The stubble on the chin is haphazard and if it's designer it's been designed by an unpaid intern on an off-day. I'm sixty. Do you know, it was all fields round here once. 'Daisy, Daisy …' Where's everybody gone?

May at last! As Uncle Charlie always used to say, 'You know you can take your cardigan off for good when there's no R in the month.' May, June, July, August: that golden quarter of the year when spring glides unto summer on the wheels of a charabanc and you forget the wild weather of March and those April days when you have to retrieve your cardigan from the wardrobe because there's a nip in the air that's rushing straight over from Cleethorpes without drawing breath. Now you can venture out into an evening that seems to last forever, or at least until tomorrow.

I got to thinking about Uncle Charlie's category of months with no R in them the other day, and I reckon May is the best, the purest, and certainly the shortest. But then I worked out that in a month like May, although there's no R, there are plenty of other letters to play with here in Yorkshire.

There are two more in the month's brief moniker, of course. M and Y. M is there for the mmms that'll be escaping the lips of people at the seaside as they lick their first proper ice cream of the year; oh, they'll have had one in March, on an ill-advised and rainy (or snowy) day trip but this feels like the real deal: the dribble down the chin, the crunch of the cornet, the sun on your back. The Y is the cry of 'Why?' from the kids when you tell them it's time to go home. You wouldn't get that in March or April: they'd scuttle back to the car faster than the Scuttling People of Starbeck used to. Now, because it's May, they just want to stay a little longer on the beach. Other letters I associate with this first R-less month are C, B, and E. C because this month is often the first glimpse I get of the sea after a winter stuck in the house: that first glimpse of those waves, that sun on that water, make me simply want to B. Well, be. Walking by a Yorkshire seascape in May is a state of bliss, I reckon. I can simply 'be' in a place like this. With ice-cream down my shirt but who cares? And the E? That's what I'll say, dragging it out as long as I can, when I settle into a café chair for a pot of tea and curd tart. Eeeee, that's lovely. That's a pot of T, of course, another letter to celebrate this month. The Qs are longer, inevitably, once this time of year gets going, but I don't really mind. Sometimes you get stuck in a Q behind a family of American tourists who keep saying G as you say EEE but that all adds to the fun. Specially when they ask for their X sunny side up and the woman behind the counter has to ask them what they mean.

The birds are out in force in May of course. Indeed, you might see a J when you're out walking in the countryside with your cousin K. You might turn to her and say, 'This is the opposite of L. This is heaven.' And she'll say I or R. Then she'll say O as a rare bird flies past to its nest. Rarer than an N, obviously.

U and I really love May, don't we? Those strolls, those times in the garden, those trips to those places that were denied to us in winter when we seemed tied to the houses by scarves and locked into hats and handcuffed by gloves.

We like this month, don't we? R. R, we do that. And so I suppose May has an R in it, after all. R it does. And then, tired by the open air, you'll go back home to ZZZ and dream of the summer. I? R!

Everybody, except the truly daft and those who think that diaries are places where you buy milk, knows about Leap Years, those shudders in the calendar where once every four years you get an extra day to enjoy coming from Yorkshire. The next one's due in 2020 and I can't wait.

Not many people in Yorkshire, though, will be celebrating 2018 as a Trip Year by singing the old traditional song on New Year's Day: 'Trip, trip, there's a song on my lip/ Trip, trip, let the year slip/before you know it next month will be here/so let's eat some parkin and drink some strong beer' and I'm sorry that the tradition of Trip Year has almost, well, tripped off the calendar.

Trip Year originated in West Yorkshire towards the end of the nineteenth century when the mills and pits and foundries and factories were in full production mode and the owners of these establishments, often sporting mutton-chop whiskers and wearing suits with waistcoats, became distressed by the fact that, in January when the weather was particularly bad, a lot of their workers couldn't get to their places of toil through the huge snowdrifts, even if they lived very close to the pit or mill. The workers who did manage to arrive were often shocked and debilitated by falling down in the snow and slipping on the ice.

An emergency meeting of the Leeds Manufacturers, Mineowners, & Millowners Association (or LMMA for short) was called at Leeds Town Hall on a freezing, foggy and sleety (or FFS for short) Friday in January to see if a solution to the problem could be thrashed out and if not, to see if some workers could just be thrashed instead.

After much general chuntering, led mainly by Obadiah

Clegg, the LMMA's honorary chunterer-in-chief, the meeting was addressed by Wilkins Wilkinson the owner of the short-lived Kippax Leather Mines. Wilkins was known by his peers as a bit of a modernist as well as a dreamer and had said at a previous meeting that he couldn't wait for the twentieth century to begin because then everybody in Yorkshire would be living in leather houses. Because of this impractical trait he wasn't taken too seriously by the rest of the LMMA but when he began to speak at the meeting and then began to explain his idea with a blackboard and some chalk they sat up and took notice, which wasn't easy for some of them.

Basically, Wilkinson suggested that January could be struck from the calendar so that February began in the hole where New Year's Day used to be; in the same way that day was added to the year in a Leap Year, then a month could disappear every other year, thus making spring come earlier and thus ensuring that more workers got to work on time and healthy. When asked why the Trip Year, as Wilkinson called it, couldn't happen every year, he pointed out that after a very short while you'd be having your Christmas dinner in summer like they did in Australia. This seemed to make sense at the time but if you examine it, it makes no sense at all.

So, for two years only, in 1897 and 1898, there was no January in certain parts of Yorkshire and you can only begin to imagine the chaos that Trip Year caused: birthdays were missed, trains failed to run, New Year's resolutions weren't begun, and Christmas turkeys suddenly seemed very old and stringy. The idea was quickly dropped and Wilkinson was drummed out of the LMMA in disgrace.

Several thousand souvenir calendars, diaries, cups and coal scuttles were produced and although many have been lost or destroyed, the few that survive can fetch huge prices on the open market or, if it's raining, in the covered market. Happy New Trip Year, everybody: maybe it wasn't such a bad idea after all!

Let's celebrate the birthday on 15th March of one of the great forgotten Yorkshiremen, Reuben Blamire of Cleckheaton, the nineteenth-century genius who invented Yorkshire Maths and who could have been as famous as

Pythagoras or Isaac Newton if only he could have worked things out properly.

Let me explain: Reuben was a greengrocer by trade but his passion was numbers. He'd sit in his parlour at night and challenge his wife Agnes to shout out fifteen numbers between one and three million and he'd add them up in three seconds. As Agnes couldn't be bothered to check if he was right or not, Reuben always assumed he was right, and maybe he was. He liked to pour boxes of currants on the ground and guess how many were scattered on the floor; he loved to gaze at flocks of passing sparrows and try to calculate how many birds were in the air.

In his grocer's shop he'd make elaborate equations from onions and carrots and he'd attempt to work out how many turnips would stretch to Heaven or Morley, whichever was furthest away. He even self-published a pamphlet, 'Blamire's Yorkshire Times Tables and Mathematical Calculations With Particular Reference To

Vegetables And Fruit', which contained several variations on traditional times tables and a number of different ways of working out dimensions using foodstuffs.

So, for instance, he created the 'Eee Times Table' around the traditional Yorkshire utterance which began 'One Eee is Eee, Two Eees are Eeee, Three Eees are Eee by Gum' and so on. The 'By Times Table' went along the lines of One By is By, two Bys are By Heck, Three Bys are By Flippin' Heck, four Bys are By Flipping Hecky Thump, right up to Twenty Bys which are 'By Flipping Hecky Thump and Me Auntie Vera's Terrier's Collar's Stud's shine' which certainly sounds more poetic and inventive than Nine Nines are Eighty One.

The mathematical calculations involved using fruit and vegetables as measuring devices, so that A Hundred and Seventeen Spuds could be the length of a cricket pitch, and Half a Leek Eaten Raw was the amount of time it took to walk from Blamire's house to the pub. The pamphlet proved a success, going into several (Sprout to the power of Cox's Orange Pippin, to be precise) printings, and Blamire's mathematical methods began to be taught in some of the more progressive local schools alongside Micklethwaite's Furniture-based Geography.

On 16th March, 1868, the day after Reuben's birthday, he began his greatest mathematical experiment, which he called Infinity By Cauliflower. The plan was to build a pile of cauliflowers so high that they would actually reach Infinity. Just before a cold and clear dawn he began to pile the cauliflowers on top of each other; he'd worked out that 324,000 cauliflowers would be enough and, of course, we know now that that number would never be enough to break the rules of physics but we're talking of an unworldly man in an innocent place at an unsophisticated time. If only he'd known that it would take millions of cauliflowers to reach anywhere near the outskirts of the foothills of infinity, he wouldn't have piled those few thousand cauliflowers in a tottering mountain. He wouldn't have climbed up rickety steps to place cauliflower on cauliflower. And he wouldn't have fired himself from a catapult to stick the last couple on the top. Witnesses said he flew through the air gracefully with a gleam in his eye and the two final cauliflowers in his hands.

He was never seen again. A rogue wind carried him far into the air, way beyond Cleckheaton until he was a Brussels sprout in the sky. Reuben Blamire, we salute you, times plum.

Last New Year's Day I went to the newsagent to buy a paper, part of a ritual that sustains me and which I feel bad about ever missing, even on freezing days. It gets me ready for the day, for the week, for the month and in this case the year. I got a paper and a magazine and I paid with a £10 note and I got an old and tired fiver in my change, and as I put it in my pocket I noticed there was something written on it in shaky handwriting in black biro. I looked closely: 'Bingley Bill', it said, and a mystery began that's come to haunt me over the last twelve months.

Who is Bingley Bill? Was the fiver intended for him? Was it a Christmas or a birthday present, did it come in a card or was it wrapped up in a pair of comedy socks? Was it part of a series of Christmas fivers given to a group of scattered friends? As well as Bingley Bill, was there

Keighley Keith and Tony from Tong? Did they get together
once a year and relive their halcyon schooldays and then
give out cards with fivers in? Or was the owner of the fiver
going to use it to pay a bill in Bingley, and he wrote on it
to remind himself? Of course, you should never write on
money but when people do it's irresistible and fascinating,
you have to admit. What was the bill he had to pay? And
was there a Settle Bill to settle and some Grassington Brass
to part with and did he write those phrases on each of the
notes? I keep saying 'he' by the way, because I'm convinced
that writing on money is the kind of daft thing that only
men would do. Women are too sensible.

I took the fiver home and determined to keep it and not
spend it; it was like a cultural object, something that I could
use to remind me in years to come of my morning walk on
the first day of a brand new year. And then I went and spent
it. I must have put in back in my pocket rather than secret-
ing it in a place of safety and now it's swimming round the
world of tills and purses and wallets and banks and Post
Offices like a fish. An old blue fish called Bingley Bill.

Where has it been, I wonder? What adventures has it
had? Has it been to a fish and chip shop in Bridlington
where it flapped in the wind and flew from somebody's
fingers and got snatched up by a passing gull who dropped
it onto an open-topped bus where it got picked up by a
little lass on her holidays who couldn't believe her eyes?

Did the little lass spend it on the biggest ice-cream you've
ever seen and then did it languish in a till for a few hours
until a business bloke got it in his change and spent it that
night in a wine bar in a West Yorkshire town? Did it go

from this point if you look closely Thomas you might see Bingley Billy searching for his fiver

DARFIELD

from the wine bar to a clothes shop and from there to a charity shop and from there to a fruit and veg stall on Doncaster market?

Did it spend a few sad weeks down the side of a settee until it got hauled out by a desperate mum looking for change? Did it fall down a grate in Otley and get washed down a river and hooked up by a fisherman hoping for a trout but glad of a fiver? Did it get washed in a pair of jeans in a Whitby washing machine and hung out to dry and did it emerge from the pocket as good as new, ready to be spent all over again?

So, if you've got Bingley Bill or if you come across it, do let me know and then I'll start the year a happy man. And it's a shame fivers can't talk, isn't it, because Bingley Bill would have a cracking story to tell. Worth every penny.

Here comes an Old Feller wandering down the main street of a Dales village; it could be any Dales village, maybe with a thwaite or an owby somewhere in the name, and the Old Feller could be any Old Feller, maybe with a Seth or a Bert somewhere in his name. The thing about this particular Old Feller in this particular Dales village is that he's whistling. He's whistling what novelists call a 'tuneless whistle', and in this case they're almost right.

Almost, but not quite. Lean closer to the Old Feller; lean even closer, through the protective whiff of Brylcreem and Sunday afternoon tap rooms. Listen to the whistling: there's a tune there somewhere. It's not just the sound of a squeaky gate or a boiling kettle or an expiring referee. It's … wait a minute, I've nearly got it, just let me get my ear right next to his puckered lips. Ah yes, there it is, a melody hiding at the back of the trills and gasps for breath: Ilkla Moor Baht 'At, the Yorkshire Anthem. Now, if you asked the Old Feller what he was whistling he might have difficulty remembering; not because he's daft but because it's the tune he always whistles, it's as natural to him as breathing. In fact, it more or less is breathing, with just a smidgeon of added sonority.

The Old Feller doesn't remember, but he learned the tune from his dad, who used to play it in the 1930s on the old piano they had in the parlour. They never went in the parlour much, only for funerals and at Christmas, and on Christmas Eve the Old Feller's dad always played Ilkla Moor Baht 'At, even though there was nothing Christmassy about it.

The Old Feller's mother always complained that it wasn't

anything like a carol, and so the Old Feller's dad would
sometimes put bits of festive music in it, so sometimes it
sounded like Where Have Them Three Kings Been Since I
Saw 'em?, or While Shepherds Sat on t' Moor by Night. The
strange thing is that if you listen to the Old Feller whistling
there's a hint of his dad's Christmas adaptations at the back
of the tune, like carol singers warbling three streets away in
a howling gale. That's how tunes get passed on, imperfec-
tions and all; for all the Old Feller knows, Ilkla Moor Baht
'At has always had a bit of tinsel in it.

Ah, but where did the Old Feller's dad learn the tune?
Well, he learned it from his Uncle Bert who used to sing in
the choir that met in the old chapel at the top end of the
dale. The Old Feller's dad used to walk with Uncle Bert up
to the chapel for choir practice and sit and listen to them
going through the songs in the years just before the First
World War. The Old Feller's dad's Uncle Bert loved
singing, but the problem was that he could only sing one
tune; every song he sang, from The British Grenadiers to
the Hallelujah Chorus, came out like Ilkla Moor Baht 'At.
For some lighter pieces of operetta or music hall songs like
My Old Man Said Follow the Van, it didn't seem to matter
too much (try it sometime: My Old Man Said Follow the
Van can indeed be sung to the tune of Ilkla Moor Baht 'At.)
but for something like a choral version of Mendelssohn's
Fingal's Cave, it didn't sound too good. Consequently, the
Old Feller's dad's Uncle Bert had to sit at the back of the
choir, with the Old Feller's dad on his knee, which is why
he only knew one song that he could pass on to his
whistling son when his son was the Young Feller not the

Old Feller. I hope you're following this family tree: there might be questions at the end. And now, wonderfully, the song is being passed on, because the Old Feller sometimes pushes his granddaughter down the street in her buggy and as he pushes, of course he whistles the only tune he ever whistles. So the other night as the Old Feller's granddaughter was going to sleep, her mum put her head round the door and she could hear the little lass in her bed humming Ilkla Moor Baht 'At, an unbroken tune going back via a Christmas parlour to a Dales chapel in the Edwardian sun.

I'll tell you what, esteemed reader, let's wander through a day in the life of a Yorkshireman and see what Lessons for Life we can learn. This day begins as a typical day but soon escalates into something quite different, as you'll see.

In what some middle-aged Yorkshiremen call the Wee

Small Hours, between Midnight and 4am, the Yorkshireman is either snoring or padding to the bathroom. He is snoring because he has left his flat cap on in the mistaken belief that it will keep his head warm during the night and therefore help him sleep. Instead, the neb has come unclicked from its mooring and has slipped and dragged the whole cap over the slumbering Tyke's face. His wife stares at the ceiling as the noise of a small nuclear reactor in meltdown issues from the torso spreadeagled next to her. Occasionally she gives the torso a poke or a deft kick but this only seems to make the snoring louder.

Lesson for Life: *Do Not Wear Your Flat Cap in Bed.*

The Yorkshireman is padding to the bathroom because he had a lovely cup of tea before bed, and a nice bottle of ale, and a tot of whisky, and now he feels what romantic novelists call an Urgent Need. He rolls out of bed and walks across the room, trying to miss each creaking floorboard but instead landing squarely on each creaking floorboard. His wife stares at the ceiling and thinks to herself that The Yorkshireman's slippers sound like the pit boots her dad used to wear.

Lesson for Life: *No Tea, no Tot, No Ale Before Bed.*

Now it is dawn, between 4am and 8am. The Yorkshireman has finally, because his flat cap fell off, fallen into a deep sleep. The alarm rings and The Yorkshireman flails around and thumps it hard, silencing it. And he goes back to sleep, dreaming of scoring a century at Headingley, snoozing so deeply that he sleeps in for a few vital minutes and the whole shape of his day is ruined. He blames the alarm clock for going off but that is like blaming the sun for rising.

Lesson for Life: *Do Not Thump The Alarm Clock. It's Only Doing Its Job.*

Now the day is speeding up and The Yorkshireman is trying to catch it. Between 9am and 12 noon he is meant to be at work but he rushes his breakfast and rushes out of the house like a cartoon character with a slice of toast in his mouth. He misses his bus and sits sulking in the bus shelter, looking so hard at the ground that he misses the next one as well. He arrives late and sweating at work and has to endure hard stares from the gaffer and 'hilarious banter' from his mates. He doesn't notice until almost twelve o'clock that there is a piece of toast the size of a 50p piece stuck in his hair.

Lesson for Life: *Do Not Run With Toast and Do Not Stare At The Ground.*

12 noon–12.30pm is The Yorkshireman's dinner hour. I know it's not an hour but this is the modern world. Normally The Yorkshireman nips out to a café and buys a sandwich and cup of tea but today he decides that he needs livening up so he nips to a different café to try an espresso for the first time in his life because he's heard they get you going. This is a mistake. The espresso almost gets him gone. He glugs the tiny splash of black fire and his eyes spring from their sockets a distance of several Yorkshire inches (like real inches, but bigger and more stylish) and his hair sticks up like an unclipped bush in a neglected park.

Lesson for Life: *There Is Never A Good Time For The Yorkshireman To Have His First Espresso.*

The rest of the day, from 12.31pm until 23.59pm, passes in an electric espresso blur for The Yorkshireman. He rushes back to work and slaps the gaffer round the ample chops. He tickles the gaffer's PA. He does a Haka by the photocopier. He feels very sleepy and extremely awake at the same time. He decides to go and get a tattoo. He decides (and this is his really big mistake) to go and get another espresso. Look up into the night sky: that's The Yorkshireman, circling the earth and laughing.

Lesson for Life: *The Yorkshireman Should Never Follow Up His First Espresso With His Second One On The Same Day.*